Charles K True

The Elements of Logic

Adapted to the Capacity of Younger Students, and Designed for...

Charles K True

The Elements of Logic

Adapted to the Capacity of Younger Students, and Designed for...

ISBN/EAN: 9783744782142

Printed in Europe, USA, Canada, Australia, Japan

Cover: Foto ©Paul-Georg Meister /pixelio.de

More available books at **www.hansebooks.com**

THE

ELEMENTS OF LOGIC:

ADAPTED TO THE

CAPACITY OF YOUNGER STUDENTS,

AND

DESIGNED FOR ACADEMIES AND THE HIGHER
CLASSES OF COMMON SCHOOLS.

By CHARLES K. TRUE, D.D.

Nihil difficile amanti.—CICERO.

REVISED EDITION.

New York:
PUBLISHED BY CARLTON & PORTER,
200 MULBERRY-STREET.
IVISON, PHINNEY & CO.,
48 AND 50 WALKER-STREET.
1861.

Entered according to Act of Congress, in the year 1860.

By CARLTON & PORTER,

in the Clerk's Office of the District Court of the United States for the Southern District of New-York.

PREFACE.

Logic, as a science, is simple and limited. Most modern treatises upon the subject have erred, by extending it beyond its proper department, on the one hand, and by excluding it from its legitimate province on the other. By some it has been made to occupy the ground of mental science or of rhetoric; by others it has been denominated, "*an* art of reasoning," as if there were any sound reasoning which is not logical, while others have claimed for it the unlimited sphere of teaching "the right use of reason." These errors have been exposed by Archbishop

Whately, and the true nature and appropriate office of logic have been explained and vindicated. His learned and able treatise has obtained favor in the universities of Great Britain and the United States, and will go far, undoubtedly, to revive and extend a neglected, but invaluable science. The principles of that work, which are none other than those of Aristotle, have been adopted as the basis of the present volume.

The treatise now presented to the public is designed for a department hitherto unoccupied.

A science, so rudimentary in its principles, and so extensive in its applications, ought to be studied with the common elements of learning. Nor, when properly explained, will it be found any more difficult to the younger student than grammar or arithmetic. It will not task the powers beyond what is desirable in salutary discipline, while its tendency to promote a habit of thinking will be greater than that of any other science. Indeed, logic must be studied early, and rendered perfectly familiar, in order to be of much practical utility in the business of life. It is so long postponed in existing systems of education, and, after all, so superficially studied, that there is scarcely one educated man in a thousand who professes to be master of logic.

This work, though simple in its arrangement, embraces all that is essential to logic, while everything which does not strictly and necessarily come within the appropriate province of the science has been excluded. Collateral matter and discursive explanations have been avoided, as rather calculated to embarrass and confuse the youthful mind. The principles and rules of the science have been stated distinctly, and illustrated by a variety of examples. If any further explanation is necessary the enlightened teacher can easily supply it. The great points will thus stand out prominently to view, and all that is added by way of comment will be associated with them in the mihd. The attention of the learner will not be distracted by many particulars, nor the memory encumbered with unessential matter.

BOSTON, *August* 14, 1840.

PREFACE TO THE SECOND EDITION.

The first edition of this book has been used chiefly in academies of a high grade and as a manual in some colleges. The improvements in this edition will make it still more acceptable to advanced students, while it will be no less adapted to the object for which it was originally designed, namely, to follow immediately after grammar in all schools where the higher branches are commenced. Will teachers of grammar schools now give this book a trial, and make known to the public the results of the experiment? Consider: Will it not be of the greatest advantage to form the habit in early life of analyzing one's process of thought in reasoning, and especially observing whether the reason given for an opinion is a general reason. For example: It is of itself no proof, that you are not at the scene of a murder, because you are here. Indeed! what other proof is necessary? Clearly *this general principle*— that no being but God can be in two places at the same time. Without this as a major premise, your alibi as a minor premise answers no purpose. To be sure this principle is implied in the minor premise, and it happens to be a sound one; but how often in practical life do we imply in our statements a general principle which is not sound; but its unsoundness escapes us, because we are not in the habit of considering it distinctively. It would be easy enough to give illustration of this from any political or religious newspaper that comes to hand. I insist, therefore, that a science so pertinent to every-day practical life should not be excluded from elementary studies, but should be taught in every grammar school.

The most important improvements in this edition are the Analytical Outline, the Chapter on Distinctions of Reasoning, and the Essay on the Philosophy of Induction.

NEW YORK, *October*, 1860.

CONTENTS.

	PAGE
ANALYTICAL OUTLINE..........................	13

PART I.—ON TERMS.

SECTION
I. DIFFERENT KINDS OF TERMS....................	23
II. OPPOSITION OF TERMS.........................	26
III. SPECIES AND GENUS..........................	28
IV. DIVISION..................................	30
V. DEFINITION................................	31

PART II.—PROPOSITIONS.

I. PARTS OF A PROPOSITION......................	35
II. DISTINCTION OF PROPOSITIONS..................	37
III. FURTHER DISTINCTIONS.......................	41
IV. DISTRIBUTION OF TERMS OF PROPOSITIONS.........	43
V. OPPOSITION................................	46
VI. CONVERSION................................	52

PART III.—ARGUMENTS.

DEFINITION OF ARGUMENTS.....................	57
I. SYLLOGISMS................................	58
II. RULES OF SYLLOGISM.........................	61
III. IRREGULAR SYLLOGISMS.......................	71
IV. HYPOTHETICAL SYLLOGISM.—DILEMMA.............	77
V. DISTINCTIONS OF REASONING...................	83

PART IV.—FALLACIES.

	PAGE
DISTINCTION OF FALLACIES	95
I. LOGICAL FALLACIES	98
II. MATERIAL FALLACIES	102

SUPPLEMENT.

I. MOODS AND FIGURES OF SYLLOGISMS	107
II. REDUCTION	114
QUESTIONS IN REVIEW	120

APPENDIX.

I. DISSERTATION ON INDUCTION	121
II. MISCELLANEOUS EXAMPLES FOR PRACTICE	152
SUPPOSED EXCEPTIONS TO RULES	168

ELEMENTS OF LOGIC.

INTRODUCTION.

ANALYTICAL OUTLINE.

1. Logic is the science of inference; it teaches how one judgment may be inferred from other judgments. To infer is to reason, hence it is usually called the science of reasoning.

2. It assumes that every mind conceives intuitively some ideas or judgments which are at once primary and certain; otherwise we could have no foundation for inference; and to infer one idea or judgment from others would give no certainty.

These ideas are called first truths. They are given by the senses, the consciousness, and the reason, and are innumerable. *I exist. There is an external world. This body is solid, ex-*

tended, round, red, warm, or cold, are first truths.

3. At first these ideas are particular, but afterward the mind unites those which are the same in some respect into classes by simple addition. This is called generalization. To express this we no longer say, *This body, and that body, and yonder body,* etc., but *body. Red body* would be a lower class made up of this red thing, that red thing, etc.

4. It is evident, furthermore, that in order to reason the mind must have some general ideas, or class ideas, that are conceived intuitively, and not formed by mere addition or generalization; for if you make a class by adding all the individuals, you gain nothing by drawing one or more out again. These general ideas are called first principles, or axioms, and are the offspring of the reason. Some of the earliest are these: *Every body is in space. No event happens without a cause. Like material causes produce like effects.*

5. It is the province of psychology to explain under what circumstances these primary ideas are given by the senses, the consciousness, and the reason; but logic assumes their existence

as the indispensable basis of inference, and its appropriate office is to explain in what way we infer one judgment from another.

6. The process of reasoning when completed is found to be simply this: *Something is predicated, that is, affirmed or denied of a class; an individual is affirmed to belong to this class, and then, of course, the same thing can be affirmed or denied of that individual.*

In whatever form a sound argument is expressed, it may always be shown to involve this process, and every unsound argument deviates from it. In reasoning we always proceed from generals to particulars, and never from particulars to generals, for this is impossible, as it would be to draw out what was never put in. A general principle, to be sure, may be inferred from one still more general; but in relation to that more general principle it is only a particular; it is a class in a class of classes—a species under a genus. For example, the general law of terrestrial gravity is an inference, not from particular instances of bodies falling to the earth, but from a more general law, which these particulars indicate. This is an instance of induction.

7. As induction has been supposed to be a mode of reasoning opposite to deduction, let us take a simple and common case. I infer that heat to such a degree as will cause the mercury in the thermometer to rise to the point marked two hundred and twelve degrees on Fahrenheit's thermometer *will always cause water to boil;* in other words, it is proved by induction to be a law of nature that *two hundred and twelve degrees Fahrenheit will cause water to boil.*

Now this conclusion is not drawn from any number of instances of the boiling of water, but from a few instances combined with the principle that *like cause will produce like effects;* for if this principle were not true, then forty thousand instances of water boiling by such a degree of heat would not prove that another case would happen, no more than finding forty thousand clovers bearing three leaves only would prove that clover always has only three leaves; or finding forty different varieties of cloven-footed animals marked with horns would prove that swine must have horns. But now I know that *like causes will produce like effects,* and I know also by observation that two hundred and twelve degrees Fahrenheit did once, or twice, or thrice cause water to boil, and I therefore infer that it will always cause water to boil. Admit the premises and the conclusion is unavoidable; and to do this is simply to affirm something of a class, then to refer an individual to that class, and then to affirm the same thing of that individual.

Now the first premise is a general principle, which is intuitively true. The only question is about the second premise, namely, whether two hundred and twelve degrees Fahrenheit was the cause of boiling in the instances observed.

You may now prove this by another argument made up of another intuitive principle, and an observed fact, or perhaps by two arguments, thus: *no event happens without a cause;* the boiling of water is an event, therefore it happened not without cause; in other words, it happened by some cause. What cause?

It is a presumption of reason *that those things which immediately and invariably precede a certain event are its cause, or include its cause.*

Now observation and experiment have shown when two hundred and twelve degrees Fahrenheit was present water invariably and immediately boiled; and when it was absent, the other circumstance remaining just as before, it did not boil. Hence it is concluded that it was the cause of the boiling in these cases.

Thus the second premise of the main argument being proved, the first conclusion is established, namely, that two hundred and twelve degrees Fahrenheit is always the cause of water boiling.

Every case of induction proper proceeds upon the same grounds and in the same way. It is, therefore, evident induction is no exception to the rule that inference is always from generals to particulars, and not from particulars to generals.

8. Reasoning by analogy proceeds in the same way; the difference is only in the character of the first premise, which is, that *similar causes are likely to produce similar effects, or that things which agree in certain attributes are likely to agree in certain other attributes.* Thus we reason by analogy that Jupiter is likely to be inhabited as well as the earth, and that retribution may be expected in a future life as well as in this.

9. Reasoning *a priori* and *a posteriori* are, not different modes of reasoning, but arguments differing in the character of one of the premises: in the one we reason from antecedents, and in the other from consequents. From the idea of perfection, as an antecedent in the human mind, Des Cartes argued *a priori* for the existence of a Perfect Being; and Paley, from the marks of contrivance in the world as an effect, proved *a posteriori* an intelligent Creator.

10. It will be seen that the value of any conclusion depends upon the degree of certainty which belongs to the premises. If they are certain the conclusion is certain; if they are probable the conclusion is only probable. This is the only distinction between mathematical and moral or practical reasoning; nor does this always exist, for some moral arguments may claim premises that are absolutely certain.

11. It remains only to observe that the syllogism is merely a certain convenient mode of stating an argument; and that is the most perfect syllogism which is framed so as to make the true process of inference the most apparent. The above instance of induction would be stated as a syllogism, thus:

Like causes will ever produce like effects.

Two hundred and twelve degrees Fahrenheit is like the cause that produced boiling of water;

Therefore, it will ever produce the like effect.

Or thus:

Whatever caused the boiling of water once will always cause it.

Heat 212° Fahrenheit caused the boiling of water once;

Therefore, it will always cause it.

12. Analyzing a syllogism, for example:

All men are mortal.
Mohammed was a man;
Therefore, Mohammed was mortal:

we find that it is made up of three propositions; that each proposition contains two terms and a copula, expressing an agreement or disagreement of the terms. Each term denotes an idea, as *all men, mortal, Mohammed;* each proposition expresses a judgment as to the relation of two terms to each other, and the last of these propositions is an inference from the other two judgments. The three operations of mind concerned in reasoning are therefore simple apprehension, judgment, and inference.

13. Language serves to express these mental operations, but the mind has ideas, judgments, and inferences before it has language, inasmuch as a sign must of necessity be subsequent to the thing signified.

14. From this analysis it appears that logic enters into the vital processes of the mind, and conducts it from the known to the unknown. A demonstration is essentially a discovery: the propositions in a book of geometry are involved in the axioms and definitions on the first page, but to draw them out is as much a discovery to the mathematician as the continent of America was to Columbus.

SYNTHESIS OF LOGIC.*

PART I.

ON TERMS.

1. THE first part of Logic treats of TERMS.

A TERM is one or more words expressing a thing, or what is thought of a thing; as,

Grass is green. *Grass* is a term, and *green* is a term.

The sun shines brightly. *The sun* is a term, and *shines brightly* is a term.

SECTION I.

DIFFERENT KINDS OF TERMS.

2. A SINGULAR TERM expresses only one individual; as,

Boston, Connecticut River, this rock, the discoverer of America.

---

* Younger students commence here.

3. A COMMON TERM is one which is not confined to a single object, as *City*, which may apply to Boston and to all other cities.

> Rock, River, Conqueror, Mariner.
> Strong, Happy, Wise, Great, Balmy, Dark.

4. A RELATIVE TERM expresses an object that is related to another object; as, *Husband*, which is related to wife. *Parent*, which implies offspring.

> Rider, Ruler, Brother, Servant, Magistrate.

5. AN ABSOLUTE TERM expresses a thing considered by itself, without reference to any other thing; as,

> River, Mountain, Power, Wisdom.

6. A POSITIVE TERM expresses a thing as actually existing; as,

> Sight, Seeing, Speech, A man speaking.

7. A PRIVATIVE TERM is one which expresses the absence of an attribute from a thing capable of it; as, *a blind man*, which denotes the absence of the power to see.

> A lame stag, A leafless oak, A dead plant.

8. A Negative Term denotes the absence of an attribute from a subject, which is not capable of it at all; as,

<blockquote>A dumb statue, Lifeless marble, Silent dews.</blockquote>

9. An Abstract Term is one which expresses a quality, without reference to any subject in which it may be found; as,

<blockquote>Roundness, Hardness, Wisdom, Justice, Folly.</blockquote>

10. A Concrete Term expresses both the attribute and the object to which it belongs; as, *wrong*, which expresses both an action and its quality; *ruler*, which indicates an agent and his office.

<blockquote>Philosopher, Governor, Wise, Energetic, Hard.</blockquote>

11. An Indefinite Term is one which does not define or mark out an object, and has the particle *not* attached to it, expressed or understood; as, *not a man*, which may imply any other being.

<blockquote>Not Brutus, Incorporeal, Unfinished, Unwise.</blockquote>

12. A Definite Term is one which does define or mark out an object and has not the particle *not* attached to it; as,

Man, Brutus, Finished, Complete, Established.

EXAMPLES.

1. Man is a rational being.
2. Cicero was a great orator.
3. This town is pleasantly situated.
4. Mothers have much solicitude.
5. Strength is acquired by exercise.
6. Far-sightedness is peculiar to seamen.
7. A dumb man is a pitiful object.
8. The silent tomb, the lifeless statue.
9. Wisdom is more precious than rubies.
10. Just and good are the laws of God.
11. The society is organized.
12. The plan is incomplete.

SECTION II.

OPPOSITION OF TERMS.

13. Consistent Terms are those which may at the same time be affirmed of the same thing; as, *dry* and *cold*.

14. Opposite Terms cannot at the same time be affirmed of the same thing; as, *black* and *white*.

The opposition of terms is fourfold.

15. Relative Opposition is that which is between relative terms, that cannot at the same time be applied to the same subject; as, *father* and *son*.

16. Contrary Opposition is that between absolute terms, that expel one another from a subject capable of either; as, *wise* and *foolish*.

17. Privative Opposition is that between a positive and privative term; as, *seeing* and *blind*.

18. Contradictory Opposition is that between a definite and indefinite term; as *Cesar* and *not Cesar*.

EXAMPLES.

1. Good and small.
2. Master and servant.
3. Ruler and subject.
4. Material and immaterial.
5. Lovely and hateful.
6. Hearing and deaf.

SECTION III.

SPECIES AND GENUS.

This subject involves no mystery, as formerly under a false philosophy.

19. SPECIES is a term that denotes a class, including several individuals; as, *Beast*, which includes the horse, cow, lion, deer, etc.

20. GENUS is a term that denotes a class, that includes several species; as *Animal*, which includes beast, bird, fish, man, insect.

A genus which cannot be comprehended under a higher genus is called *highest genus;* and a species which includes no lower species is called *lowest species.*

21. THE ESSENTIAL DIFFERENCE denotes an essential part of a species that distinguishes it from other species; as *rational*, which is the essential difference of the species man, because it is the essential part of man that distinguishes him from beast, bird, etc.

22. A PROPERTY is something necessarily joined to the essential difference; as *power of laughing*, which is the property of man as a rational being.

23. An Accident is something that may be, or may not be joined to the essential difference, as *tall* or *short*, *living in London*, *born in Paris*.

EXAMPLES

1. This tree is a Pine, with very thick boughs.
2. This is a small magnet, having the power of attraction, and it turns upon a pivot in a direction north and south.
3. This vessel is a ship, having three masts, full rigged, and very long.
4. A republic is a government in which the people have sway and choose their own rulers.
5. This seminary of learning is a college.
6. A lame animal, a blind stag.
7. General terms are names of classes.
8. A bird with blue feathers and broad wings.
9. Mercury is the planet nearest the Sun.
10. A circle is a figure whose circumference is in every part equally distant from the center.
11. A whale is the largest of fish, and is often seen in our waters.

12. A plant is an organized being, destitute of sensation.

SECTION IV.

DIVISION.

24. DIVISION is the distinct enumeration of the several things signified by a term; as,

New England is divided into Maine, New Hampshire, Vermont, Massachusetts, Rhode Island, and Connecticut.

Bark signifies the rind of a tree, a small ship, and the cry of a dog.

25. RULE OF DIVISION. *The several parts must not be contained in one another, and all together must be exactly equal to the thing divided.*

EXAMPLES.*

1. The year is divided into Summer, Autumn, Winter, and Spring.
2. Metals are divided into gold, copper, and iron.
3. The Human race is divided into Americans, Africans, Asiatics, Chinese, and Europeans.

* Examples, it will be seen, are given for criticism.

4. King signifies a ruler and also a man's name.

5. Mercury is the name of a heathen deity, a planet, a plant, and quicksilver.

6. The globe consists of land and water.

7. Form signifies shape and ceremony.

8. Trump is a trumpet and a winning card.

9. Orchard is an inclosure for apple-trees and fruit-trees.

10. A solid body has length and breadth.

11. A tree consists of trunk, branches, and leaves.

SECTION V.

DEFINITION.

26. A DEFINITION is an expression explaining a term, so as to distinguish or separate it from everything else.

27. A NOMINAL DEFINITION distinguishes the meaning of a term by an equivalent term, which is better known; as,

>Decalogue—the Ten Commandments.

When all the equivalent terms are given it is one kind of division.

28. A Physical Definition lays down the real parts of the essence; as,

> Injustice is the intentional violation of another's rights.
> A plant has leaves, stalks, roots.

This last is another kind of division.

29. A Logical Definition assigns the Genus and the Essential Difference of the thing defined; as,

> Man is a rational animal.

30. Accidental Definition, or Description, assigns the accidents or properties of the thing defined; as,

> Man is an animal that uses fire to dress his food.
> Columbus was a native of Genoa.

31. It will be observed that more than one of these kinds of definition will coincide in matters strictly scientific.

32. Rule of Definition. *A Definition must be adequate, that is, not too extensive nor too narrow, for the thing defined; plainer, and contained in a suitable number of proper, not figurative terms.*

33. The chief concern of Logic with defini-

tions is, that words be not used in *different senses* in argument.

EXAMPLES.

1. Pleiades—the seven stars.
2. A king is the ruler of a people.
3. A square is a figure having four sides and four right angles.
4. Surprise is a state of mind produced by some unexpected occurrence.
5. A circle is a figure whose circumference is in every point equally distant from the center.
6. Species is a term for a class.
7. Wine is the juice of the grape.
8. Whiteness is the color arising from the prevalence of brightness.
9. A plant is an organized being destitute of sensation.
10. Logic is the science of inference.
11. Man is a risible animal.
12. Mercury is the planet nearest the Sun.
13. A Church is a congregation of faithful men, in which the word of God is preached, and the ordinances duly administered.

14. Punishment is pain inflicted for a crime, in order to correct the offender.

15. Courage is boldness and endurance in time of peril.

16. Sin is voluntary transgression of a known law.

17. Sin is any transgression of God's law.

PART II.

OF PROPOSITIONS.

The second part of Logic treats of Propositions.

SECTION I.

1. A PROPOSITION is a judgment expressed in words, or a sentence, whereof one part is affirmed or denied of the other; as,

> Man is an animal.
> Moses and Thomas are not Statesmen.
> All animals are mortal.

2. The Subject of a proposition is that part, of which something is affirmed or denied; as, in the last example *all animals* is the subject.

3. The Predicate of a proposition is that which is affirmed or denied of the subject; as, in the same example, *mortal* is the predicate.

4. The Copula is the verb by which the two terms are connected. It is the present tense of the verb *to be*, with or without the particle *not*.

5. Sometimes one part of a proposition is contained in another; as, *the wind blows, I think;* which imply, *I am thinking, the wind is blowing.*

6. The subject of a proposition usually stands first, and the predicate last; but this order is sometimes inverted, as,

<blockquote>In the West are extensive Prairies.</blockquote>

EXAMPLES.

1. Matter is divisible.
2. Man is not infallible.
3. Christopher Columbus was the discoverer of America.
4. A wise man rules his own spirit.
5. George Washington was a brave but prudent general.
6. The world exhibits marks of a great convulsion.
7. I see—he feels—you walk—they run.
8. All tyrants deserve death.
9. Blessed are the pure in heart.

SECTION II.

DISTINCTION OF PROPOSITIONS.

7. PROPOSITIONS are distinguished into affirmative and negative, which is a distinction with respect to Quality.

8. AN AFFIRMATIVE PROPOSITION is one in which the predicate is declared to agree with the subject; as,

> Man is a fallible creature.

9. A NEGATIVE PROPOSITION is one in which the predicate is declared to disagree with the subject; as,

> The world is not eternal; no miser is happy.

10. Propositions are also distinguished into Universal and Particular, which is a distinction in respect to Quantity.

11. A UNIVERSAL PROPOSITION is one in which the predicate is asserted of the whole of the subject.

The signs of universality are *all*, *every*, *no*, *neither*, and the like, which are expressed or understood; also, proper names, as John, London; and common names with a singular or a definite sign; as, *That boy, five books.*

> No discontented man is happy.
> Those stars revolve about the sun.

EXCEPTIONS. In negative propositions the idiom of the English language makes *all* and *every* particular or singular terms; as, *all the sailors were not drowned,* does not mean that all the sailors escaped drowning, but that some of them only escaped drowning; or, it denies drowning of the totality as a collective unit.

To state a universality here you must say: *None of the sailors were drowned,* or simply, *The sailors were not drowned.*

12. A PARTICULAR PROPOSITION is one in which the predicate is asserted of an indefinite part of the subject.

The signs of particularity are *some, many, few, several,* and the like; as,

> Some culprits were not punished.

13. A UNIVERSAL AFFIRMATIVE PROPOSITION is one in which the predicate is said to agree

with the *whole* of the subject; as, in the above example—*All men are mortal.* This is not only a universal proposition, but a universal affirmative proposition.

All tyrants deserve death.

14. A UNIVERSAL NEGATIVE PROPOSITION is one in which the predicate is said to disagree with *the whole* of the subject; as, *no discontented man is happy;* which is not only a universal proposition, but a universal negative proposition.

No sins are excusable.

15. A PARTICULAR AFFIRMATIVE PROPOSITION is one in which the predicate is asserted to agree with only some part of the subject; as, *some islands are fertile;* which is not only a particular proposition, but a particular affirmative proposition.

Several men were drowned.

16. A PARTICULAR NEGATIVE PROPOSITION is one in which the predicate is asserted to disagree with only some part of the subject; as, *some culprits were not punished;* which is not only

a particular proposition, but a particular negative proposition.

17. A, E, I, O are symbols employed to represent these propositions: thus,

A stands for universal affirmative.
E stands for universal negative.
I stands for particular affirmative.
O stands for particular negative.

EXAMPLES.

1. These sailors were not drowned.
2. Paris is a gay city.
3. Some animals are sagacious.
4. Men are unaccountable beings.
5. Every effect must have an adequate cause.
6. Few men become suddenly rich.
7. Many criminals are not brought to punishment.
8. Planets are bodies moving in orbits about the sun.
9. Islands are surrounded by water.
10. The Christian religion is attested by miracles.
11. Every sinner will be punished.

12. That man was the inventor of lightning rods.
13. Not all his foes could alarm him.
14. No flower is always in bloom.
15. All laws are not useful.
16. Every soldier was not killed.

SECTION III.

FURTHER DISTINCTIONS OF PROPOSITIONS.

18. Propositions are distinguished into Categorical and Hypothetical.

19. The Categorical asserts simply that the predicate agrees or disagrees with the subject; as,

>Truth is invaluable.
>The eye is a natural telescope.

20. The Hypothetical asserts with a condition, or with an alternative; as,

>If it storms, the ship will not sail.
>It is summer or winter.

21. Hypothetical Propositions are divided into Conditional and Disjunctive.

22. A Conditional Proposition is one whose parts are limited by the particle *if*, or some word expressing a condition; as,

> If there be no fire, there will be no heat.
> Cesar deserved death, if he was a tyrant.

23. A Conditional Proposition contains two, and only two, Categorical Propositions, whereof one follows from the other.

> If the Bible is true, it ought to be studied.

The first is called the antecedent, and that which results from it is called the consequent.

24. A Disjunctive Proposition asserts that a subject agrees with one of two or more predicates, or a predicate with one of two or more subjects; as,

> It is either day or night.
> Prosperity or adversity will be your lot.

25. A Disjunctive may easily be converted into a Conditional; thus,

> It is either day or night.
> If it is not day, it is night.

EXAMPLES.

1. Man is free, or he is not responsible.
2. This proposition is either true or false.
3. The earth must move, if the sun be fixed.
4. If the harvest is large, corn will be cheap.
5. If there be no providence, prayer avails not.
6. If the boat goes, the letter will probably reach him before morning.
7. Wisdom is the principal thing, if Solomon is right.
8. Either the sun or the moon will be eclipsed that day.
9. If logic is useful, it deserves to be studied.
10. If Cromwell was an Englishman, he was a usurper.

SECTION IV.

DISTRIBUTION OF THE TERMS OF PROPOSITIONS.

26. A Term is said to be distributed when it is taken universally or in its utmost extent, so as to stand for everything to which it is capable of being applied, that is, for each of its significates; and undistributed when it stands for an

indefinite portion only of the things signified by it, that is, for an indefinite part of a class. In the following example the subject is distributed and the predicate undistributed.

All birds are animals.

In the following the predicate is distributed and the subject undistributed.

Some birds are not web-footed.

It is evident that the whole class of *web-footed* are separated by the *not* from *some birds*.

RULE I.

27. *Subjects are distributed in all universal and no particular propositions.*

All men are mortal.
Great Britain rules the ocean.
Wicked men are not wise.
The fixed stars twinkle.
No miser is a happy man.

RULE II.

28. *Predicates are distributed in all negative and no affirmative propositions.*

No virtue is *an evil.*
Some rich men are not *good men.*

A distributes the subject, O the predicate, I neither, and E both.

N. B.—A definite portion of a class is a small class, and the term which expresses it is distributed.

>   Most men are poor.
>   These men are rich.

Rule II has some EXCEPTIONS in what logicians call *unnatural propositions*, such as,

All triangles are *all* figures bounded by three straight lines.
Some stars are *all* the planets.
Some stars are not *some* planets.

But these being noted by the form of expression will make no difficulty.

I do not see with Sir William Hamilton sufficient reason, in such exceptions, to revolutionize the established forms of logic.

EXAMPLES.

1. Many ships were lost in the gale.
2. The storm did not last long.
3. Most Americans can read.
4. All the laws were not enforced.

5. Everything in the political world looks dark.
6. No good man can hate his brother.
7. Every sin is a violation of the divine law.
8. All visible things had a beginning.
9. Some difficult things are not evils.
10. Charity never faileth.
11. Charity suffereth long and is kind.
12. Five men were shipwrecked.

SECTION V.

OPPOSITION OF PROPOSITIONS.

29. Two propositions are said to be opposed, which, having the same subject and predicate, yet differ in quantity, or quality, or both; as,

A. All islands are fertile,
I. Some islands are fertile, } in quantity.

A. All islands are fertile,
E. No island is fertile, } in quality.

A. All islands are fertile,
O. Some islands are not fertile, } in both.

E. No island is fertile,
I. Some islands are fertile, } in both.

30. With any given subject and predicate, four distinct propositions may be stated, namely, A, E, I, and O, any two of which may be said to be opposed; as,

    A. Every disease is contagious.
    E. No disease is contagious.

Or,

    I. Some diseases are contagious.
    O. Some diseases are not contagious.

31. There are four different kinds of opposition.

32. CONTRARY OPPOSITION is when a universal affirmative is opposed to a universal negative; as,

    A. All human inventions are perfect.
    E. No human invention is perfect.

33. SUBCONTRARY OPPOSITION is when the particular affirmative is opposed to the particular negative; as,

    I. Some human inventions are perfect.
    O. Some human inventions are not perfect.

34. SUBALTERN OPPOSITION is when a universal affirmative is opposed to a particular affirm-

ative, or a universal negative to a particular negative; as,

    A. Every human invention is perfect.
    I. Some human inventions are perfect.

Or,

    E. No human invention is perfect.
    O. Some human inventions are not perfect.

35. CONTRADICTORY OPPOSITION is when the universal affirmative and the particular negative are opposed, or the universal negative and the particular affirmative; as,

    A. Every human invention is perfect.
    O. Some human inventions are not perfect.

Or,

    E. No human invention is perfect.
    I. Some human inventions are perfect.

36. Four conditions are requisite to constitute a contradiction, namely, to speak of the same thing: (1.) In the same sense; (2.) In the same respect; (3.) With regard to the same third thing; and, (4.) At the same time. If any of these be wanting, *is* and *is not* may agree. As,

1. *An opinion is and is not faith.* It is an inoperative and unacceptable belief; it is not an effectual and saving faith. 2. *Troilus is and is not red-haired.* He is with respect to his head; he is not with respect to his beard. 3. *Socrates is and is not long-haired,* he is in comparison with Scipio; he is not in comparison with Xenophon. 4. *Solomon was and was not a good man.* He was in his youth; he was not in his middle age.

THE RULES OF OPPOSITION.

RULE I.

37. CONTRADICTORY PROPOSITIONS are always the one true and the other false; as,

    A. All men are mortal.
    O. Some men are not mortal.

    E. No tyrant deserves death.
    I. Some tyrants deserve death.

RULE II.

38. CONTRARY PROPOSITIONS may be both false, but never both true; as,

50   ELEMENTS OF LOGIC.

A. Every disease is contagious.
E. No disease is contagious.

RULE III.

39. SUBCONTRARIES are never both false, but they may be both true.

I. Some amusements are innocent.
O. Some amusements are not innocent.

RULE IV.

40. SUBALTERNS are sometimes both true, sometimes both false, and sometimes one is true and the other false; as,

A. Every defensive war is just.
I. Some defensive wars are just.
E. No crime is an evil.
O. Some crimes are not an evil.
A. Every measure of government is wise.
I. Some measures of government are wise.

Diagram showing the relation of the four judgments: A E I O.

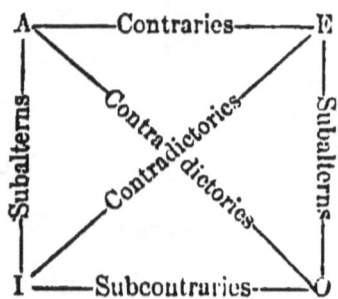

EXAMPLES.

1. Some horses are unruly.
   Some horses are not unruly.

2. No intolerant men are good men.
   Some intolerant men are good men.

3. All pleasures are hurtful.
   Some pleasures are not hurtful.

4. All hopes are consoling.
   Some hopes are consoling.

5. No virtuous man is ungrateful.
   Some virtuous men are ungrateful.

6. All islands are fertile.
   Some islands are fertile.

7. All animals are mortal.
   All animals are not mortal.

8. Every patriot is a Christian.
   Some patriots are not Christians.

9. Some diseases are contagious.
   All diseases are contagious.

10. All laws are not useful.
    Some laws are not useful.

SECTION VI.

CONVERSION OF PROPOSITIONS.

41. A proposition is said to be converted, when its terms are transposed and the truth preserved; as,

> Some painters are poets.
> Some poets are painters.

42. The proposition to be converted is called the ORIGINAL, that into which it is converted the CONVERSE; as,

> *Original.* No reptile is a quadruped.
> *Converse.* No quadruped is a reptile.

43. SIMPLE CONVERSION is where the subject and predicate simply change places; as,

> Some boasters are cowards.
> Some cowards are boasters.

44. PARTICULAR CONVERSION is where, in transposition, the converse requires a particular term to preserve the truth of the original; as,

> All swallows are birds.
> Some birds are swallows.

45. Rule. *In all cases the converse must be truly implied by the original, and no term must be distributed in the converse that was not distributed in the original.* Hence,

> A. All men are mortal;
> All mortals are men,

is not proper conversion, for A distributes the subject only, (28) but *mortal* is the predicate, therefore its distribution in the converse, namely, *all mortals*, is unwarranted.

46. The converse of a universal affirmative proposition is a particular affirmative; or, more briefly, A is converted into I.

> A. All men are mortal.
> I. Some mortals are men.

47. The converse of a universal negative is a universal negative—E into E; as,

> E. No deer is an elephant.
> E. No elephant is a deer.

48. Particular affirmative propositions are converted only into the same—I into I; as,

> I. Some infidels are learned men.
> I. Some learned men are infidels.

49. A particular negative is inconvertible; as,

    O. Some birds are not swallows.

You cannot say,

    O. Some swallows are not birds;

Or,

    E. No swallows are birds;

For these are negative propositions, and distribute the predicate, (28) which is *birds;* but, in the original, *birds,* is not distributed. (27.)

Some logicians teach that the particular negative may be converted by considering the particle *not* attached to the predicate, by which the proposition is taken as an affirmative.

Some statesmen are not wise, may be stated:

    Some statesmen are not-wise.

This you may convert simply:

    Some not-wise, that is, unwise, are statesmen.

In like manner a universal affirmative may be simply converted by changing its quality; thus,

    All good reasoners are candid men,

may be converted into

    None but candid men are good reasoners.

CONVERSION OF PROPOSITIONS.

This is called conversion by contraposition.

50. EXCEPTIONS. Universal affirmatives may be converted simply when the predicate by some word notifies its distribution, contrary to rule, sec. iv, 28, and when it is understood to be exactly equal to the subject, as in definitions, etc.

All men are [all] rational animals.

So some particular negative proposition may be converted simply when the predicate notifies its non-distribution. See exceptions to Rule II, Sec. iv, 28.

Some elms are not some trees.

EXAMPLES.

1. All Britons are freemen.
2. Some Britons are freemen.
3. No unhappy man is a perfect Christian.
4. Some fish are not salmon.
5. Some orators are not statesmen.
6. No offensive wars are righteous enterprises.
7. Every learned man is a thankful man.
8. Some great geniuses are ignorant men.
9. Some parrots are not talkers.

10. Every true Christian is a patriot.
11. Some angels are sinners.
12. Some amusements are hurtful.
13. All birds have feathers and wings.
14. All equiangular triangles are equilateral.
15. Some stars are all the planets.
16. Some stars are not some planets.
17. A few men are not all the voters.
18. Some birds are not like some birds.

PART III.

OF ARGUMENT.

1. THE third part of Logic treats of Argument, or reasoning expressed in words.

2. AN ARGUMENT is an expression in which, from something laid down and granted as true, something else beyond this must be admitted to be true, as following necessarily from the other. That which is laid down is called the Premises, that which results therefrom is called the Conclusion.

3. Every valid argument must conform to the Logical axiom, that being the only principle on which all reasoning proceeds, namely: *Whatever is universally affirmed or denied of a class, may be affirmed or denied, in like manner, of everything comprehended in that class.*

Or, as stated by Aristotle, and hence called Aristotle's dictum:

Whatever is predicated of a term distributed may be predicated in like manner of everything contained in it. As,

> All tyrants deserve death;
> Cesar was a tyrant;
> Therefore Cesar deserved death.
>
> No man enslaved by appetite can be happy;
> The sensualist is enslaved by appetite;
> Therefore, no sensualist can be happy.

SECTION I.

OF SYLLOGISM.

4. An argument stated at full length and in its regular form is a SYLLOGISM. The above examples are syllogisms.

5. Every regular syllogism contains three, and only three terms, called the Minor term, Major term, and Middle term.

> All *tyrants deserve death.*
>   3   2
> *Cesar* was a *tyrant,*
>   1   3
> Therefore, *Cesar deserved death.*
>   1   2

6. The subject of the conclusion is the minor term; the predicate of the conclusion is the major term; and the other term with which these are compared is the middle term; as,

>All tyrants deserve death;
>*Middle.*
>Cesar was a tyrant;
>*Minor. Major.*
>Therefore Cesar deserved death.

The predicate of the conclusion is called the major term on account of its being naturally more extensive than the subject. By the rule it is undistributed in affirmative propositions, that is, it has applications beyond the subject. Part II, Sec. iv, 28.

In the example, *deserving death* is applicable to many besides Cesar.

7. Every regular syllogism contains three, and only three propositions, called the Major premise, the Minor premise, and the Conclusion.

8. THE MAJOR PREMISE is that in which the major term is compared with the middle term.

>*Major Premise.* All tyrants deserve death;
>Cesar was a tyrant;
>Therefore, Cesar deserved death.

9. THE MINOR PREMISE is that in which the minor term is compared with the middle term; as,

                All tyrants deserve death;
Minor Premise. Cesar was a tyrant;
                Therefore, Cesar deserved death.

10. THE CONCLUSION is that in which the major and the minor terms are compared together.

              All tyrants deserve death;
              Cesar was a tyrant;
Conclusion. Therefore, Cesar deserved death.

11. In every regular syllogism the major premise is placed first, the minor next, and the conclusion last.

EXAMPLES.

1. All the faithful are dear to God;
Some that are afflicted are faithful;
Therefore, some that are afflicted are dear to God.

2. No work that exhibits marks of design can be the effect of chance;
The world exhibits marks of design,
Therefore, the world cannot be the effect of chance.

3. That which improves the mind is useful;
Study improves the mind;
Therefore, study is useful.

4. No literary production is perfect.
This treatise is a literary production;
Therefore, this treatise is not perfect.

5. Every vegetable is combustible;
Every tree is a vegetable;
Therefore, every tree is combustible.

SECTION II.

THE RULES OF SYLLOGISM.

12. The validity of all arguments may be tested by the logical axiom (3); and no syllogism is valid which does not conform to it.

13. It cannot, however, always be directly and conveniently applied; as, for example, in the following valid syllogism:

> No virtues are evils;
> All virtues are difficult; therefore,
> Some difficult things are not evils.

This syllogism may be altered by converting the minor premise, and then it will plainly appear to conform to the logical axiom; thus,

No virtues are evils;
Some difficult things are virtues; therefore,
Some difficult things are not evils.

14. But to avoid the inconvenience of altering a syllogism, in order to apply the logical axiom, logicians have adopted the following canons and rules by which to test the validity of syllogisms.

15. CANON I. *If two terms agree with one and the same third, they agree with each other.*

16. CANON II. *If one term agrees and the other disagrees with one and the same third, these two disagree with each other.*

This agreement must be understood to be that kind of class relation explained by the logical axiom, and required by Aristotle's dictum, otherwise the canons will mislead.

Silver is a mineral;
Platina is a mineral;

Will not prove that platina is silver, though these terms agree with the term mineral.

All studies which tend to increase national and private wealth are useful;
The studies at Oxford do not tend to increase national and private wealth;
Therefore, the studies at Oxford are not useful.

This might at first seem to be founded on canon II, but it is a fallacy, as is easily seen in a case precisely parallel.

> All cultivated plants grow;
> The wild rose-bush is not cultivated;
> Therefore, the wild rose-bush does not grow.

John Jones is sentenced to die;
The first private in the ranks is John Jones;
Therefore, the first private in the ranks is sentenced to die.

Here the first canon is observed, but the logical axiom is not complied with unless you consider proper names as distributed and standing for a class of one. See Part II, Sec. ii, 11; and Sec. iv, 28. Strictly this is rather a case of identification than of inference.

To avoid error, we must add to the two canons the following six rules or cautions:

RULE I.

17. *Every syllogism must have three, and only three terms, and three, and only three, propositions.*

Ambiguous terms are to be considered as two terms.

The following example has, in reality, four terms:

Repentance is a good thing;
Wicked men abound in *repentance;*
Therefore, wicked men abound in a good thing.

If the word *repentance* be regarded as having the same meaning in both premises, then one proposition or the other is false.

Ambiguous terms are fruitful sources of error in argument.

Sometimes an argument will appear to have too many terms when a little alteration, not affecting the sense, will show but three; thus:

No irrational agent could produce a work which manifests design;
The universe is a work which manifests design;
Therefore, no irrational agent could have here produced the universe;

This seems to have five terms, but the first premise is properly:

A work that manifests design could not be produced by an irrational agent.

RULE II.

18. *The middle term must be distributed once at least in the premises.*

The following example violates the rule:

> Granite is a mineral;
> Lead is a mineral;
> Therefore, lead is granite.

The middle term *mineral* is undistributed; hence, *granite* is compared to *mineral* in a part of its extension, and *lead* is compared to it in another part of its extension; therefore, neither of the canons of logic are complied with, for the two extremes are not compared to one and the same third.

The following seems to violate the rule:

> True patriots are disinterested;
> Few men are disinterested;
> Therefore, few men are true patriots.

But by putting the minor premise in another form, and transposing the premises, it would stand thus:

> Disinterested men are few;
> True patriots are disinterested;
> Therefore, true patriots are few.

RULE III.

19. *No term must be distributed in the conclusion, which was not distributed in one of the premises.*

The following violates the rule:

> Some diseases are contagious;
> No rheumatic fevers are contagious;
> Therefore, rheumatic fevers are not diseases.

Here you employ the term *diseases* in the whole of its extent in the conclusion, while you employ it in only a part of its extent in the premise.

RULE IV.

20. *Two negative or two particular premises prove nothing.* As,

> Slate is not a metal.
> Flint is not a metal.

Here two terms disagree with a third. This is not according to the canons, which requires either that both should agree with the third, or one agree and the other disagree.

> Some bad men are eloquent orators;
> Some good men are eloquent orators;
> Therefore, some good men are bad men.

THE RULES OF SYLLOGISM. 67

Here you have the middle term undistributed, which is contrary to Rule 2, and therefore, not according to the canons.

> Some bad men are eloquent orators;
> Some good men are not eloquent orators;
> Therefore, some good men are not bad men.

This is contrary to Rule 3.

The following syllogism with negative premises may be made regular by considering one of them an affirmative:

> No man is happy who is not secure;
> No tyrant is secure;
> Therefore, no tyrant is happy.

> No man who is insecure is happy;
> Every tyrant is insecure;
> Therefore, no tyrant is happy.

RULE V.

21. *If either premise be negative or particular, so also is the conclusion.* As,

> No virtuous man is a rebel;
> X and Y are virtuous men;
> Therefore, X and Y are not rebels.

Here one term is said to disagree with a middle and the other to agree, hence they disagree with each other, and the conclusion must be negative.

> All who study diligently deserve reward;
> Some scholars study diligently;
> Therefore, some scholars deserve reward.

Here is a particular premise, and you cannot draw anything but a particular conclusion, for a universal conclusion would be contrary to Rule 3, and against the canons.

The following in form violates the first part of this rule, but it might be stated so as to be regular.

> None but candid men are good reasoners.
> Few infidels are candid;
> Therefore, few infidels are good reasoners.

It may be changed thus:

> All good reasoners are candid;
> Most infidels are not candid;
> Therefore, most infidels are not good reasoners.

Or thus:

> Those who are uncandid are not good reasoners;
> Most infidels are uncandid;
> Therefore, most infidels are not good reasoners.

EXAMPLES.

1. No one is free who is enslaved by his appetites;
A sensualist is enslaved by his appetites;
Therefore, a sensualist is not free.
2. All gold is precious;
This mineral is precious;
Therefore, this mineral is gold.
3. All wise legislators adapt their laws to the genius of the people;
Solon adapted his laws to the genius of the people;
Therefore, Solon was a wise legislator.
4. All pious men desire the freedom of their country;
Thomas Paine desired the freedom of his country;
Therefore, Thomas Paine was a pious man.
5. Warm countries alone produce wine;
Spain is a warm country;
Therefore, Spain produces wine.
6. Some poisons are vegetables;
No poisons are useful drugs;
Therefore, some useful drugs are not vegetables.

7. They who subvert the foundations of morality ought not to be respected;
Atheists subvert the foundations of morality;
Therefore, Atheists ought not to be respected.

8. All vegetables grow;
This animal grows;
Therefore, this animal is a vegetable.

9. Most men are poor;
Most men are intelligent;
Therefore, some intelligent men are poor.

10. Light is contrary to darkness;
Feathers are light;
Therefore, feathers are contrary to darkness.

11. An enslaved people is not happy;
The English are not an enslaved people;
Therefore, the English are happy.

12. None but whites are civilized;
The Ancient Germans were whites;
Therefore, they were civilized.

13. None but whites are civilized;
The Hindoos are not whites;
Therefore, they are not civilized.

14. None but civilized people are white;
The Gauls were white;
Therefore, the Gauls were civilized.

SECTION III.

IRREGULAR SYLLOGISMS.

22. THE ENTHYMEME is a defective syllogism, having one premise suppressed; as,

> Christianity teaches the way to future happiness;
> Therefore, it should be diligently sought.

Here the major premise is suppressed. Supply it, and the syllogism is complete; thus,

> Whatever teaches the way to future happiness should be diligently sought;
> Christianity teaches the way to future happiness;
> Therefore, Christianity should be diligently sought.

> Every man is mortal;
> Therefore, every king is mortal.

Here the minor premise is omitted. (9.)

Frequently the conclusion is stated first; thus,

> Enthusiasm should be avoided,
> Because it leads astray from reason.

23. A regular syllogism may be changed into an Enthymeme by simply suppressing one of the premises, or by stating the conclusion first, and joining thereto one of the premises by the conjunction *for*, *as*, or *because*. As,

> Whatever enables us to overcome difficulties is useful;
> Perseverance enables us to overcome difficulties;
> Therefore, perseverance is useful.

This may be changed to Enthymeme, thus:

> Whatever enables us to overcome difficulties is useful;
> Therefore, perseverance is useful.

Or thus:

> Perseverance enables us to overcome difficulties;
> Therefore, perseverance is useful.

Or thus:

> Perseverance is useful, for it enables us to overcome difficulties.

Or thus:

> Perseverance is useful; for,
> Whatever enables us to overcome difficulties is useful.

24. To reduce an Enthymeme to a syllogism, observe first what is the conclusion or point

established. This contains the minor and major terms, (10) and the remaining term must be the middle term. Having these, the syllogism may be easily constructed according to the rules (Sec. I.) by supplying the implied premise.

In the last example, *perseverance is useful*, is the conclusion. Consequently the remaining term, *enables us to overcome difficulties*, is the middle term. (6.) *Perseverance enables us to overcome difficulties* is implied, and makes the minor premise. (9.)

25. THE SORITES is a continued argument, consisting of a series of propositions arranged in such a manner that the predicate of each forms the subject of the following proposition, except the concluding, which takes the subject of the first proposition; as,

> There can be no enjoyment of property without government;
> No government without laws enforced;
> No laws enforced without a magistrate;
> No magistrate without obedience;
> And no obedience where every one acts as he pleases; therefore,
> There can be no enjoyment of property where every one acts as he pleases.

26. Every Sorites contains as many syllogisms as there are propositions intervening between the first and the last proposition.

>The English are a brave people;
>A brave people are free;
>A free people are happy;
>Therefore, the English are happy.

This may be broken up into two syllogisms, thus:

>A brave people are free;
>The English are a brave people;
>Therefore, the English are free.

>A free people are happy;
>The English are a free people;
>Therefore, the English are happy.

27. THE EPICHIREMA is a compound argument, of which one or both the premises are separately proved before the conclusion is drawn. As,

>Unjust laws endanger the stability of government, *for they create discontent among the people;*
>Laws restraining freedom of conscience are unjust, *for they require the people to abandon their dearest concerns;*
>Therefore, laws restraining freedom of conscience endanger the stability of government.

28. Irregular syllogisms are the most commonly employed in discourses of every kind; for the regular form of syllogism would not often consist with elegance of style, nor is it often requisite to produce conviction.

EXAMPLES.

1. The mind is a thinking substance;
   A thinking substance is a spirit;
   A spirit has no composition of parts;
   That which has no composition of parts is indissoluble;
   That which is indissoluble is immortal;
   Therefore, the mind is immortal.
2. He is a good man, therefore he is happy.
3. He is a miserable man, because he is vicious.
4. Whatever tends to subvert government should be deprecated;
   Therefore, civil dissensions should be deprecated.
5. Every man is an animal;
   Every animal is a living creature;
   Every living creature is a substance;
   Therefore, every man is a substance.

6. A religion attested by miracles is from God, for none but God can suspend the laws of nature, and God would not permit them to be suspended but for his glory.

The Christian religion was attested by miracles, for the friends and the enemies of Christianity have agreed in declaring it was;

Therefore, the Christian religion is from God.

7. No opinion that tends to immorality should be embraced.

Atheistical sentiments tend to immorality;

Therefore, atheistical sentiments should not be embraced.

8. It is lawful for one man to kill another who lies in wait to kill him, for the laws of nature and the customs of mankind sanction it;

Clodius lay in wait to kill Milo, for his equipage, arms, guards, movements, etc., prove it;

Therefore, it was lawful for Milo to kill Clodius.

9. With some of them God was not well pleased, for they were overthrown in the wilderness.
10. He that is of God heareth my words; ye therefore hear them not, because ye are not of God.
11. Men are free agents, for they are accountable beings.
12. Skepticism is an enemy to man, since it is an enemy to truth.

SECTION IV.

HYPOTHETICAL SYLLOGISMS — DILEMMA.

HYPOTHETICAL SYLLOGISMS are of two kinds: Conditional and Disjunctive.

29. A CONDITIONAL SYLLOGISM is one in which the major premise is a conditional proposition; as,

If there is a God, this world is governed by a providence;
But there is a God;
Therefore, this world is governed by a providence.

30. The clause containing the condition is called the ANTECEDENT, that containing the assertion is called the CONSEQUENT.

31. Rule. *If the antecedent be granted so is the consequent, if the consequent be denied so is the antecedent; but not vice versa; that is, the antecedent being denied proves nothing, and the consequent being granted, proves nothing;* as,

> If Samuel is a father he has authority;
> But Samuel is a father;
> Therefore, he has authority.

> If Samuel is a father he has authority;
> But he has not authority;
> Therefore he is not a father.

But *vice versa*, the argument is not valid.

> If Samuel is a father he has authority;
> But Samuel is not a father;
> Therefore, he has not authority.

But he might have authority from some other relation or office. Again,

> If Samuel is a father he has authority;
> But he has authority;
> Therefore, he is a father.

32. Conditional Syllogisms may be reduced to regular syllogisms, by considering the antecedent the subject, and the consequent the predicate of an universal affirmative proposition.

If the Atheists are right the world exists without a cause;
But the Atheists are not right;
Therefore, the world does not exist without a cause.

Reduced thus:

The case of the Atheists being right is the case of the world existing without a cause;
But the present case is not the case of the Atheist being right;
Therefore, the present case is not the case of the world existing without a cause: (See Rule 3, Sec. ii.)

33. A DISJUNCTIVE SYLLOGISM is one whose major premise is a disjunctive proposition.

The earth either moves in a circle or an ellipse.
But the earth does not move in a circle;
Therefore, it moves in an ellipse.

It is either spring, summer, autumn, or winter;
But it is not summer, autumn, or winter;
Therefore, it is spring.

34. Disjunctive syllogisms are easily convertible into conditional, and so brought under the foregoing rules; as,

If the earth does not move in a circle it moves in an ellipse;
But it does not move in a circle;
Therefore, it moves in an ellipse.

35. THE DILEMMA is a complex conditional syllogism, of which the major premise contains two or more conditional propositions, and the minor a disjunctive proposition; as,

If A is B, C is D, and if E is F, G is H;
But either A is B or E is F;
Therefore, C is D or G is H.

If Æschines joined in the public rejoicings he is inconsistent; if he did not he is unpatriotic;
But Æschines either did or did not join in the public rejoicings;
Therefore, he is either inconsistent or unpatriotic.

The advantage of the Dilemma is this: that you may not be able to affirm or deny any proposition, but you may always state it disjunctively. Demosthenes might not be able to prove that Æschines did join in the public rejoicing, or that he did not join; but certainly he did or he did not. .

This Dilemma may easily be reduced to two

or more conditional syllogisms and these to regular syllogisms.

36. Thus all hypothetical syllogisms as well as all other arguments may be reduced to regular syllogisms, and so subjected to the test of the logical axiom. But it is more convenient in ordinary practice to try them by their own rules.

EXAMPLES.

1. If this man has a fever, he is sick;
But he is sick;
Therefore, he has a fever.

2. The world was created by chance, or by an intelligent agent;
But it was not created by chance;
Therefore, it was created by an intelligent agent.

3. If Louis Philippe is a good king France is likely to prosper;
But Louis Philippe is a good king;
Therefore, France is likely to prosper.

4. If C be not the center of the circle some other point must be;
But no other point can be the center;
Therefore, C is the center of the circle.

5. If this man were wise he would not speak irreverently of the Scriptures in jest; if he were good, he would not do so in earnest;
But he does it either in jest or in earnest;
Therefore, he is either not wise or he is not good.

6. If logic is useless it deserves to be neglected;
But logic is not useless;
Therefore, it does not deserve to be neglected.

7. Either money or produce will be scarce in the market;
But produce will not be scarce;
Therefore, money will be scarce.

8. If W. were a general he would have power;
But W. is not a general;
Therefore, he has not power.

9. If W. be a general he must be obeyed;
But W. must be obeyed;
Therefore, he is a general.

SECTION V.

DISTINCTIONS OF REASONING.

1. The divisions of reasoning into Deduction and Induction, Mathematical and Moral, Demonstrative and Probable, by Analogy, A priori, A posteriori, A fortiori, Reductio ad absurdum, and Reductio ad impossibile, are only different ways of laying down premises, the process of reasoning being always the same, namely, deductive—from generals to particulars.

The degree of certainty in the conclusion, when the process of inference is correct, depends upon the degree of certainty in the premises.

2. In PURE MATHEMATICAL REASONING, the principles and judgments being always self-evident, the conclusions are absolutely certain; in MIXED MATHEMATICS self-evident axioms and judgments are mixed with matters of fact and measurements of instruments, to which some uncertainty is attached; consequently the same uncertainty attaches to the conclusion.

EXAMPLE.

If a straight line meet another straight line, the sum of the adjacent angles will be equal to two right angles.

Suppose the straight line D C meets the straight line A B at the point C; then will the angles A C D and D C B together be equal to the two right angles A C E and E C B.

Axiom.—A whole is equal to the sum of all its parts.

A C D is a whole of which A C E and E C D are its parts.

Therefore, A C D is equal to all its parts, namely, A C E and E C D.

Axiom.—If equals be added to equals the sum is equal;

D C B added to A C D, and D C B added to A C E plus E C D are equals added to equals.

Therefore, the sum is equal.

Now, as A C E is one of the right angles in question, you have only to prove that the other two angles E C D and D C B equal the other right angle E C B.

DISTINCTIONS OF REASONING. 85

The sum of all the parts is equal to the whole.
E C D plus D C B are all the parts of the angle E C B.
Therefore, they are equal to the whole E C B.

Thus you have proved that D C B added to A C D is equal to A C E added to E C B.

This is a case of pure mathematics, because I have supposed D C a straight line meeting another A B; but if I take a rod and make a line between two points on a field, I do not know that it is in reality a perfectly straight line. Hence, there is a mixture of practical uncertainty, with the absolute certainty of the axioms employed in any calculation about it; hence, such calculation is called mixed mathematics.

3. INDUCTION is a course of argument by which, from the principles of causation, joined with particular phenomena, we infer the general law of those phenomena.

Some of the principles of causality are the following: *No event, no phenomenon happens without a cause. Like material causes produce like effects. No cause can operate where it is not.*

From the principles we directly infer the postulate: *The immediate and invariable antecedent of any phenomenon may be presumed to be its cause or contain its cause.*

In respect to spiritual agencies the principles of causation are the same, except in relation to the will, whose distinguishing characteristic is freedom. Of this alone we cannot predicate that like causes will produce like effects. We cannot certainly know how it will behave under any circumstances.

It should be observed, that it may be beyond human power to perceive, when any physical change takes place, what the real cause is; but we know that it must be found where the event takes place, and that the invariable and immediate antecedent of the event must contain it.

To discover the cause, therefore, of any phenomenon, we must observe under what circumstances that phenomenon happens and notice its invariable antecedent.

Having done this we are prepared to make the proper inference, and the whole process can be put into a syllogism with the particular cause, as discovered in one or two cases, for a minor premise, and a principle of causation for a major premise. The principles of causality

DISTINCTIONS OF REASONING.

are intuitively true, like the axioms of mathematics; hence, induction has the same certainty as mixed mathematics.

EXAMPLE.

The law of magnetic attraction, or that the magnet will always attract iron, is proved thus:

A material cause will always produce the same effect.

Or, more particularly,

Whatever is the cause of the attracting of iron in one or two cases will always attract iron;
A magnet is the cause of attracting iron in one or two cases;
Therefore, it will always attract iron.

Now how do we know that it was the magnet and not something else that caused the iron to move?

We must make several experiments, and apply the following rule:

RULE FOR OBSERVATION.

If a phenomenon be preceded by anything, so that when that thing is present in different circumstances that phenomenon takes place, but does not take place when that thing is absent, though the circumstances remain the same, then that thing is the cause of the phenomenon or contains the cause.

This rule will show, on making a few experiments, that the magnet is the cause of the attraction of iron.

Some things will not admit of the latter part of the rule being applied, as matter, gravitation, electricity, etc., can never be absent from any event in this world.

This rule in its two parts may be symbolically exhibited thus:

Part I.—A B C.   A D E.
          a b c.   a d e.

Let *a* represent a phenomenon, and A something supposed to be its cause. In one case A has the circumstances or adjuncts B C, in the other case different circumstances, D E. Now *a* appearing with A in different circumstances shows the latter to be its cause.

Part II.—Now, if we have A B C.   B C,
                                a b c.   b c,
this will show the absence of *a* when A is absent, though the circumstances which attended A remain the same.

Sometimes the particular cause is obtained by testimony or revelation, and you have only to supply the major premise. Thus, we know God predicted contingent events in the prediction concerning the sins of Judas and Peter, and from this we prove his absolute foreknowledge.

In this case the arguments would stand thus:

Whoever can predict contingent events foreknows all things.
God has predicted contingent events;
Therefore, God foreknows all things.

To prove the minor premise we may say—

Human transgressions are contingent events;
God has predicted human transgressions in the case of Judas and Peter;
Therefore, God has predicted contingent events.

By induction the psychologist discovers distinctions between the powers of the mind; for example, that sensation and perception cannot give the idea of space, but some other power called intuition or the reason.

4. REASONING FROM ANALOGY is arguing with premises made up of principles and judgments respecting similar things, or things that are alike in some attributes. This definition would include induction, as treated by most writers on

the subject; but I consider the difference to be very important, because the principles on which Induction is based are certainties, but those of Analogy are but probabilities.

Some of the principles on which reasoning by Analogy is based are:

Similar causes will be likely to produce similar effects.

Things that resemble each other in certain attributes will be likely also to resemble each other in some other attributes.

An attribute found in several individuals belongs to a class. [This is the old principle of induction.]

Thus, horned animals have cloven hoofs, is a law in natural history, and is proved thus:

Animals that resemble each other in some attributes are likely to resemble each other in other attributes;
All horned animals resemble the ox, sheep, etc., in being horned;
Therefore, they will be likely to resemble them in other attributes as having cloven hoofs.

In the following example the conclusion disagrees with facts:

An attribute of a, b, and c clovers is likely to belong to the whole class;
Having three leaves is an attribute of a, b, and c clovers,
Therefore, it is likely to belong to the whole class.

5. REASONING A PRIORI is reasoning from antecedents to consequents. Thus, the idea of God, the perfect and infinite One, is proved true by the pre-existing ideas of infinity and perfection.

>Every necessary and universal idea of the human mind must indicate a reality;
>The ideas of the perfect and infinite are necessary and universal in the human mind;
>Therefore, they indicate a reality.

6. REASONING A POSTERIORI is reasoning from consequents to antecedents.

>Whatever exhibits marks of design proves an intelligent author;
>The world exhibits marks of design;
>Therefore, the world proves an intelligent author.

7. REASONING A FORTIORI is inferring a judgment from premises which have already been admitted to prove a point less probable.

>If robbery deserves imprisonment, much more does highway robbery.
>If God foresees contingent events he must foresee necessary events.

8. Reductio ad absurdum is proving that a certain proposition is true, because its contradiction involves an absurdity.

9. Reductio ad impossibile is proving a proposition to be true by showing that its contradiction is inadmissible.

These are often employed in mathematics.

10. Probable reasoning is drawing inferences from premises that are not certain, but more or less probable.

When both premises are of this character then the result is not so probable as either premise, but as a fraction of one of them.

Thus, if the probability of the arrival of ocean mail to-day may be represented by $\frac{2}{3}$, and the probability of your receiving letters by it is $\frac{1}{2}$, then the probability of your receiving letters to-day is but $\frac{1}{2}$ of $\frac{2}{3}$, that is, $\frac{1}{3}$.

The rule is to represent the probability of each premise as compared with certainty by a fraction, and multiply these fractions together for a result.

EXAMPLES.

1. Thirty-two degrees Farenheit will always freeze water.

DISTINCTIONS OF REASONING. 93

2. Swans are white.
3. Jupiter is inhabited.
4. If one straight line cross another straight line the opposite angles are equal.
5. The freedom of the will is proved by the idea of liberty.
6. The shadow of the earth upon the moon proves that it is round.
7. If highway robbery and murder deserve death, piracy deserves death.
8. A certain reporter is generally correct, say five times out of six. A certain statement is probably his report, the probability being represented by two fifths, what is the probability of the report being true?
9. If the probability of your winning a game be one half, what is the probability of your winning three games in succession?
10. The law of terrestrial gravitation is proved by an apple falling to the ground.
11. A certain degree of attention is necessary to memory, as experience demonstrates.
12. Swine have horns, if what is true of individuals is true of a class.

13. This servant will always return in due season, because he always has done so.
14. The emperor will declare war, because he never submits to a national insult.
15. The will is free, and therefore its future acts are unknown by even an infinite mind.
16. Retribution may be expected in a future state, judging from the effects of virtue and vice in this life.
17. The will never acts without some motive, and therefore, if you know a man's motives in any case, you may know how he will choose.
18. This case is typhus fever, for it exhibits many symptoms of that disease.
19. Mercury, Venus, and the Earth are opaque, and therefore all the planets are opaque.
20. The bull-dog, terrier, mastiff, etc., bark; therefore, all dogs bark.
21. Quadrupeds, birds, fishes, etc., have a nervous system; therefore, all animals have a nervous system.

PART IV.

OF FALLACIES.

1. The fourth part of Logic treats of Fallacies.

2. A Fallacy is an unsound argument of any kind.

3. Fallacies are of two kinds; logical fallacies and material fallacies.

4. I. Logical Fallacies are those which in form violate any of the rules of syllogism.

In these the error is entirely in the process of reasoning, and the conclusion does not follow from the premises; as,

> Every rational agent is accountable;
> Brutes are not rational agents;
> Therefore, brutes are not accountable.

This violates the third rule of syllogism.

5. II. Material Fallacies are those which in form do not violate any of the rules of syl-

logism, but the premises either are not wholly true in fact, are unduly assumed, or result in a conclusion not relevant to the question which is argued.

In material fallacies the fault is entirely in the matter of the propositions, and not in their form or connection.

> All bodies move toward the center of the universe;
> All bodies move toward the center of the earth;
> Therefore, the center of the earth is the center of the universe.

In this example there is no fault in the process of reasoning; the conclusion results from the premises, but the minor premise contains a statement which is not true in fact.

☞ Some logicians make a third division of fallacies into semi-logical, including those made by ambiguous terms: for if these terms are used in two senses they make a logical fallacy; and if they are used in only one sense they make a material fallacy; and you cannot always tell which. A simple instance is the following:

> Light is contrary to darkness;
> Feathers are light;
> Therefore, feathers are contrary to darkness.

6. Fallacies are rarely presented in the syllogistic form. They are usually found in enthymemes, and the error lurks in the suppressed proposition.

Sometimes they are offered in the form of questions so stated that a false conclusion will be likely to be implied.

7. Whately remarks, All jests are fallacies. They tend to excite laughter by betraying their fallacious character while putting on the air of serious argument. The contrast amuses. For example: A gentleman seeing a young man whom he knew going by with a looking-glass, cried out, "Ah, Joseph, don't carry that glass about, it will *reflect* on you." This, reduced to a syllogism, will be found to violate the first rule of syllogism, by having an equivocal *middle*.

8. To determine whether an argument be valid or fallacious, let the following directions be followed.

RULE.

Reduce the argument to a syllogistic form. If it be found incapable of taking that form it is of course a fallacy. If it be reducible to a syllogism, observe carefully the import and the number of its terms and propositions, and apply the rules of syllogisms. If it violates any of them it is a logical fallacy. If not, observe if either of the premises be untrue or inadmissible, or the same as the conclusion, or result in a conclusion different from the one required. If so it is a material fallacy.

SECTION I.

LOGICAL FALLACIES.

9. It is evident that logical fallacies are as numerous as are the ways of violating the five rules of syllogism.

Most of those made by ambiguous terms may be classified as follows:

10. I. THE FALLACY OF EQUIVOCATION, arising from an equivocal word, or from the ambiguous structure of the sentence.

This class will be found to violate the first rule of syllogism; as,

> All that believe shall be saved;
> The devils believe;
> Therefore, the devils shall be saved.

> Every one desires happiness;
> Virtue is happiness;
> Therefore, every one desires virtue.

In the first example the term *believe* is equivocal, having two different senses. There is, therefore, in reality, two terms; and the syllogism, consequently, has four terms, which is contrary to Rule I of syllogisms. In the second example the minor premise is ambiguous.

11. II. THE FALLACY OF SIMILAR EXPRESSION arises from words that are derived from the same root and are similar in sound, but not in sense; such as *art, artful; faith, faithful; design, designing.* As,

> Designing men should be avoided:
> This man has many designs;
> Therefore, he should be avoided.

This violates Rule I of syllogism, for there are in reality four terms.

12. III. THE FALLACY OF COMPOSITION OR DIVISION is when the middle term is used collectively in one premise, and not collectively, but distributively, in the other. As,

> Two and three are even and odd;
> Five is two and three;
> Therefore, five is even and odd.

This is a fallacy of composition. *Two and three* is the middle term, and it is used distribatively in the major premise, and collectively in the minor premise. Hence there are properly four terms in this argument, which is contrary to Rule I of syllogism.

> The planets are seven;
> Mercury and Venus are planets;
> Therefore, Mercury and Venus are seven.

This is a fallacy of division. The middle term is used distributively in the minor premise, and collectively in the major.

13. IV. THE FALLACY OF ACCIDENT is when the middle term is understood simply and as to its essence, in one premise, but in the other is so used as to imply that something, which does not belong to it essentially, but *accidentally*, is taken into account with it. As,

> Whatever is bought in the shambles is eaten by man;
> Raw meat is bought in the shambles;
> Therefore, raw meat is eaten by man.

Here the middle term is *bought in the shambles*, and it is used in the minor premise, as considered simply, and as to its essence; but in the major premise it should be understood in connexion with something else, as, *when prop-*

erly cooked. Hence, four terms are employed in reality in this argument which violates Rule I of syllogism.

EXAMPLES.

1. No one is rich who has not enough;
    No miser has enough;
    Therefore, no miser is rich.
2. All that glitters is not gold;
    Tinsel glitters;
    Therefore, tinsel is not gold.
3. He who calls you a man speaks truly;
    He who calls you a fool calls you a man;
    Therefore, he who calls you a fool speaks truly.
4. Warm countries alone produce wine;
    Spain is a warm country;
    Therefore, Spain produces wine.
5. What we eat grew in the fields;
    Loaves of bread are what we eat;
    Therefore, loaves of bread grew in the fields.
6. What is universally believed is true;
    The existence of a God is true;
    Therefore, the existence of a God is universally believed.

7. Whatever is universally believed must be true;
The immortality of the soul is not universally believed;
Therefore, it is not true.

8. What I am you are not;
But I am a man;
Therefore, you are not.

SECTION II.

MATERIAL FALLACIES.

14. Material fallacies may be as numerous as errors of reasoning, mistakes of judgment, or willful duplicity can make them.

The most common may be included in the following classes:

15. I. THE FALLACY OF BEGGING THE QUESTION is that of inferring a conclusion from premises substantially the same as the conclusion, or depending upon the conclusion; as when we attempt to prove a thing by itself, or by a synonymous word, or by something which is itself to be proved by the very point you seek to establish. As,

God is eternal, because he is without beginning or end.
Opium produces sleep because it is soporific.

We know the Scriptures are true from the infallible testimony of the Church, and we know the Church is infallible by the declaration of the Scriptures.

The last example is what is called reasoning in a circle.

16. II. THE FALLACY OF FALSE ASSUMPTION is when the premises are unduly or unwarrantably assumed; as when we attempt to prove a thing by something that is false, or unknown, or partially stated. As,

All bodies that move themselves are animated;
All stars and heavenly bodies move themselves;
Therefore, the stars and all the heavenly bodies are animated.

Meteors have a volcanic origin;
For they cannot otherwise be accounted for.

We hold this doctrine to be true by the authority of St. Paul in such and such texts.

This is a fallacy, if these texts do not contain the whole of the apostle's testimony to the point in question, and is sometimes called the fallacy of partial reference.

17. III. THE FALLACY OF MISTAKING THE QUESTION is that in which the premises are such as

result in a conclusion different from the one required, but apparently the same. As,

> Alfred the Great was a scholar;
> For he founded the University of Oxford.

18. The sophist will not always draw out the conclusion, but leave it to be inferred, for in that case its irrelevancy will be less likely to be detected.

19. This fallacy is often conveyed in appeals to prejudice, to the passions, or to personal considerations; sometimes in the form of objections, and sometimes by implication, in arguments, which go to prove a part of what is required. As,

> Gentlemen of the jury, this man is a friend to the rights of the people. Will you convict him?
>
> This work is not evangelical. Look at the statements made in the eighth chapter. Are these warranted by the New Testament?
>
> These objections are many and weighty. Can such a science be worthy of credit?

EXAMPLES.

1. The soul occupies the whole body, for it resides in every member.

MATERIAL FALLACIES. 105

2. The plant is capable of much growth, for it has great vegetative powers.
3. The soul suffers dissolution with the body at death. See Ecc. iii, 18, 19, 20; Job xxxiv, 15; Psa. cxlvi, 3, 4.
4. The Bible cannot be the rule of faith, for men understand it very differently.
5. We may expect some dreadful disaster, for the sky last night was full of falling meteors.
6. The appearance of strange birds flying south in the highest northern latitudes which have been explored, and of floating plants, as well as men who declare by signs that they come from the far north, indicate that the earth is concave about the poles, and the interior of the earth is inhabited.
7. Mohammed is a prophet, for the Koran declares it; and the Koran is true, for Mohammed received it from God, as he affirms.
8. Whatever is contrary to experience is not to be believed.
   Miracles are contrary to experience;
   Therefore, miracles are not to be believed.

9. Paul was not a Roman citizen, for he was born at Tarsus in Cilicia.
10. Job was a great sinner, for he was overwhelmed with great calamities.
11. No evil should be allowed that good may come of it;
All punishment is an evil;
Therefore, no punishment should be allowed that good may come of it.
12. No man can possess power to perform an impossibility;
A miracle is an impossibility;
Therefore, no man can possess power to perform a miracle.
13. Which of you having an ox or an ass fall into a pit, will not pull him out on the Sabbath day?
The last is a personal appeal, called *Argumentum ad hominem*, and is allowable when your object is to silence the captious. As offered to prove the point in question, it is a fallacy. (19.)

SUPPLEMENT.

SECTION I.

MOODS AND FIGURES OF SYLLOGISMS.

This subject may be advantageously studied after the scholar has become perfectly familiar with the foregoing, and is expert in the application of all the rules of logic. In that case it may serve to discipline the mind, otherwise it will only perplex. One may be an able logician without the doctrine of moods and figures.

1. The Mood of a Syllogism is the designation of the quantity and quality of its propositions.

This is done by the symbols A, E, I, and O, which stand respectively for the universal affirmative, universal negative, particular affirmative, and particular negative.

The following, for example, is A, A, A.

    A. All animals are mortal;
    A. All men are animals;
    A. Therefore, all men are mortal.

The following is E, A, E.

    E. No human invention is perfect;
    A. Language is a human invention;
    E. Therefore, no language is perfect.

2. The whole number of the moods of valid syllogisms is only eleven. A, A, A,—A, A, I,—A, E, E,—A, E, O,—A, I, I,—A, O, O,—E, A, E,—E, A, O,—E, I, O,—I, A, I,—O, A, O.

3. As there are sixty-four different ways in which it is possible for A, E, I, O to be combined to form a syllogism, there might be fifty-three other moods formed, as E, E, A,—I, I, I, etc.; but they would offend against one or more of the five rules of syllogism. As,

    I. Some birds are animals;
    I. Some fish are animals;
    I. Therefore, some fish are birds.

    E. No human invention is perfect;
    E. No language is perfect;
    A. Therefore, language is a human invention.

These examples are contrary to the fifth rule of syllogisms. Two negative or two particular premises prove nothing.

4. THE FIGURE OF A SYLLOGISM denotes the situation of the middle term, in respect to the major and minor terms.

5. FIGURE FIRST is when the middle term is the subject of the major premise and the predicate of the minor premise. As,

A. Every wicked man is miserable;
A. Every tyrant is a wicked man;
A. Therefore, every tyrant is miserable.

E. No discontented man is a happy man;
A. Every wicked man is a discontented man;
E. Therefore, no wicked man is a happy man.

A. All the faithful are dear to God;
I. Some that are afflicted are faithful;
I. Therefore, some that are afflicted are dear to God.

E. No virtue is an evil;
I. Some difficult things are virtues;
O. Therefore, some difficult things are not evils.

6. To this figure the logical axiom applies directly; and to this figure all the other figures may be reduced.

7. Figure Second is when the middle term is the predicate of both the major and the minor premises; as,

   E. No happy man is discontented;
   A. Every wicked man is discontented;
   E. Therefore, no wicked man is a happy man.

   A. Every wicked man is discontented;
   E. No happy man is discontented;
   E. Therefore, no happy man is a wicked man.

   E. No evil is a virtue;
   I. Some difficult things are virtues;
   O. Therefore, some difficult things are not evils.

   A. Every good man is afflicted;
   O. Some rich men are not afflicted;
   O. Therefore, some rich men are not good men.

8. Figure Third is when the middle term is the subject of both the premises. As,

   A. All the faithful are dear to God;
   A. All the faithful are afflicted;
   I. Therefore, some that are afflicted are dear to God.

   I. Some of the faithful are afflicted;
   A. All the faithful are dear to God;
   I. Therefore, some that are dear to God are afflicted.

MOODS AND FIGURES OF SYLLOGISMS. 111

A. All the faithful are dear to God;
I. Some of the faithful are afflicted;
I. Therefore, some that are afflicted are dear to God.

E. No virtue is an evil;
A. All virtues are difficult;
O. Some difficult things are not evils.

O. Some called Christians are not true believers;
A. All called Christians profess faith;
O. Therefore, some who profess faith are not true believers.

E. No virtue is an evil;
I. Some virtues are difficult.
O. Therefore, some difficult things are not evils.

9. FIGURE FOURTH is when the middle term is the predicate of the major and the subject of the minor premise.

10. This is the reverse of the first figure and is the most awkward of all. As,

A. Every tyrant is a wicked man;
A. Every wicked man is miserable;
I. Therefore, some that are miserable are tyrants.

A. Every wicked man is discontented;
E. No discontented man is happy;
E. Therefore, no happy man is a wicked man.

I. Some afflicted are faithful;
A. All the faithful are dear to God;
I. Therefore, some that are dear to God are afflicted.

E. No evil is a virtue;
A. All virtues are difficult;
O. Therefore, some difficult things are not evils.

E. No evil is a virtue;
I. Some virtues are difficult;
O. Therefore, some difficult things are not evils.

11. Each of the eleven allowable moods will not go in every figure, for it will violate some of the rules of syllogism in one figure, though not in another. For example, A, A, A, which goes in the first figure will not go in the third figure.

Figure 1st. All wicked men are miserable;
           All tyrants are wicked men;
           Therefore, all tyrants are miserable.

Figure 3d. All wicked men are miserable;
           All wicked men are tyrants;
           Therefore, all tyrants are miserable.

This violates Rule III of syllogism, for the term *tyrants* is distributed in the conclusion, though not in the premises. Besides, the minor premise is incorrect.

12. Some of the moods, also, which might be admitted in some of the figures are useless, as having a particular conclusion when the universal might be drawn.

For example, A, A, I will go in the fourth figure, but in the first figure it is useless.

Figure 4th. A. Every tyrant is a wicked man;
            A. Every wicked man is miserable;
            I. Therefore, some that are miserable are tyrants.

Figure 1st. A. Every wicked man is miserable;
            A. Every tyrant is a wicked man;
            A. Therefore, every tyrant is miserable.

But,
            I. Therefore, some tyrants are miserable:

would be a useless conclusion, for a universal conclusion is legitimate.

13. For these reasons, out of the forty-four allowable moods, which mighty possibly go into the four figures, only nineteen are retained. Examples of all the nineteen are found above under the definitions of the four figures.

14. To assist in remembering these moods, and the figure in which they are found, the following mnemonic lines have been invented:

First. bArbA'rA, cElA'rEnt, dArI'I, fErI'O.
Second. cEsA'rE, cAmE'strEs, fEstI'nO, bArO'kO.
Third. dArA'ptI, dIsA'mIs, dAtI'sI, fElA'ptOn, bOkA'rdO, fErI'sO.
Fourth. brAmA'ntIp, cAmE'nEs, dImA'rIs, fEsA'pO, frEsI'sOn.

Here, it will be seen, are only ten moods; but some are employed in more than one figure, as E, I, O, making nineteen in all the four figures.

15. If any syllogism be not found in these lines it cannot be a valid syllogism; it is a logical fallacy.

16. The utility of the mnemonic lines is like that of duly certified weights and measures, by which we test the size or weight of bodies without the necessity of a minute and tedious calculation.

SECTION II.

REDUCTION.

17. The process by which the moods of the last three figures are changed into a mood of the first figure is called REDUCTION.

18. This is done in two ways; by Ostensive Reduction and by Reductio ad impossibile.

19. Ostensive Reduction is performed by the conversion of one of the premises, A into I, E into E, I into I, and by transposing the premises when occasion requires.

For example, take Cesare of the second figure.

 cEs. No happy man is discontented;
 A. Every wicked man is discontented;
 rE. Therefore, no wicked man is a happy man.

This may be converted into Celarent of the first figure by the simple conversion of the major term, thus:

 cE. No discontented man is a happy man;
 lA. Every wicked man is a discontented man;
 rEnt. Therefore, no wicked man is a happy man.

Take now Camestres of the second figure and convert that also into Celarent. To do this you will only have to convert the minor premise and transpose the premises, as will be seen in the following examples.

 cAm. Every wicked man is discontented;
 Es. No happy man is discontented; *(convert and transpose.)*
 trEs. Therefore, no happy man is a wicked man.

cE. No discontented man is a happy man;
1A. Every wicked man is discontented;
rEnt. Therefore, no wicked man is a happy man.

20. In like manner all the moods of the last three figures can be reduced into one of the four perfect moods of the first figure.

21. In the mnemonic lines the initial letters *b, c, d, f*, show to which mood of the first figure the reduction is made, namely, *barbara, celarent, darii*, or *ferio*. The letter *m* signifies that the premises are to be transposed, as above, in *Camestres;* the letter *s* denotes that the proposition, which the preceding vowel stands for, is to be converted by simple conversion, and *p*, by particular conversion; but *p* in *Bramantip* marks that the premises, when changed, warrant a universal conclusion instead of a particular. The symbols A E I O mark the moods, that is, the quality or quantity of the propositions.

22. REDUCTIO AD IMPOSSIBILE is when you reduce a mood to the first figure, by substituting the contradictory of the conclusion for one of the premises; by which an absurdity follows which proves not directly that the conclusion is true, but that it cannot be false.

Thus *Baroko,* in the second figure,

bAr. Every good man is afflicted;
Ok. Some rich men are not afflicted;
O. Therefore, *some* rich men are not good men.

bAr. Every good man is afflicted;
bA. All rich men are good men;
rA. Therefore, all rich men are afflicted.

Which conclusion is notoriously false, and the original conclusion which you had drawn is, therefore, true.

23. The letter *k* in the mnemonic lines denotes that the proposition indicated by the vowel immediately preceding is to be substituted by the contradictory of the conclusion; the other letters, not above explained, have no signification.

EXAMPLES.

1. Whoever has reflection and volition has the essential properties of mind;
Mankind has reflection and volition;
Therefore, mankind has the essential properties of mind.

2. Whatever is universally believed must be true;
The existence of God is not universally believed;
Therefore, it is not true.

3. Whoever is capable of deliberate crime is responsible;
An infant is not capable of deliberate crime;
Therefore, an infant is not responsible.

4. Some philosophers reckon virtue good in itself;
The Epicureans did not reckon virtue good in itself;
Therefore, the Epicureans were not philosophers.

5. Prudence has for its object the benefit of individuals;
But prudence is a virtue;
Therefore, some virtue has for its object the benefit of individuals.

6. Whatever is expedient is conformable to nature.
Whatever is conformable to nature is not hurtful to society.
Therefore, what is hurtful to society is never expedient.

7. No man is happy who is not secure;
No tyrant is secure;
Therefore, no tyrant is happy.

8. All true patriots are friends to religion;
Some great statesmen are not friends to religion;
Therefore, some great statesmen are not true patriots.

9. All true Christians have peace;
Some afflicted men are true Christians;
Therefore, some afflicted men have peace.

10. No uncandid man is fit to reason correctly;
Some infidels are uncandid;
Therefore, some infidels are not fit to reason correctly.

11. E, E, E,—I, O, O,—I, E, O.

12. I, A, I,—A, E, E, in the first figure.

13. A, A, A in the third figure, A, E, O.

QUESTIONS IN A GENERAL REVIEW.

1. What is Logic?
2. What does it assume as its foundation?
3. What are first truths?
4. What are first principles?
5. What is the true process of reasoning?
6. What is Aristotle's dictum?
7. What is a distributed term?
8. What are the rules of distribution?
9. What is opposition?
10. What is conversion?
11. What two canons have logicians inverted to test the validity of arguments?
12. What six rules must be observed?
13. What are hypothetical syllogisms?
14. What two kinds of these?
15. Can they be reduced to one?
16. Can they be reduced to categoricals?
17. What is a dilemma.
18. What is the special advantage of it?
19. What distinctions of reasoning are found?
20. Are these different in principle?
21. What division of fallacies is made?

APPENDIX.

I.

THE PHILOSOPHY OF INDUCTION.*

It has long been the fashion to decry the logic of Aristotle, because, its legitimate use not being understood in the medieval schools, it served to divert the minds of men from the study of nature, and set them whirling about in dialectic circles to educe the principles of science and the laws of the universe; and Bacon and Des Cartes have been lauded to the skies, because they taught that nature reveals her laws only in the passing phenomena of matter and mind, as presented to the senses and the consciousness, which must be carefully analyzed

---

* First delivered before the Philosophical Society of Dickinson College. 1853.

and then generalized by the process of induction. A comparison has been made between the organon of Aristotle and the organon of Bacon, or, to speak more precisely, between the method of deduction and of induction, altogether to the disparagement of the former, until at length it has come to pass that it is no longer regarded by many as of vital importance to scientific investigation, while induction is considered as not merely an indispensable auxiliary to the discovery of new truths and principles, but as the only fundamental process of inference—the only process by which, from facts perceived by the intelligence, you can advance to the determination of the laws and principles which are the objects of science.

It is remarkable that, notwithstanding the exaltation of induction, since Bacon directed the attention of philosophers to it, no thorough attempts were made to expound its philosophy and to institute its canons until very recently. Dr. Whewell, Mr. John Stuart Mill, Dr. Henry Tappan, and Sir William Hamilton, and writers in other tongues, have supplied the desideratum by works profoundly investigating the whole subject of logic, and particularly induction.

We have, therefore, the means by which we may sit in judgment upon the question and render an enlightened verdict.

COUSIN'S VIEW OF INDUCTION.

The particular aspect of the question which it is the design of this paper to examine, is clearly presented in the following remarks in Cousin's critique of the philosophy of Locke. Cousin wonders, as well he may, that a leader in the sensual and Baconian school of philosophy should so far be warped from his appropriate sphere of thought as to lose sight altogether of induction as one of the legitimate modes of knowledge, while, at the same time, casting contempt upon the syllogism as the proper type of the reasoning process!

"Thus intuition and demonstration are the different modes of knowledge, according to Locke. But are there no others? Have we not knowledge which we acquire neither by intuition nor demonstration? How do we acquire a knowledge of the laws of external nature? Take which you please, gravitation for instance. Certainly there is no simple intuition and immediate evidence here, for experiments multiplied and combined are necessary to give the slightest law; and even this will not suffice, since the slightest surpasses the number, whatever it be, of experiments from which it is drawn. There is need, therefore, of an intervention of some other operation of mind besides intuition. Is it demonstration? Impossible, for demonstration is the perception of the relation between two ideas by means of a third; but it is upon the condition that the latter should be more general than the two others, in order to embrace and connect them. To demonstrate is, in the last analysis, to deduce the particular from the general. Now, what is the more general physical law from which gravitation can be deduced? We have not deduced the knowledge of gravitation from any other knowledge anterior to it, and which involves it in the germ. How, then, have we acquired this knowledge, which we certainly have? and, in general, how do we acquire the knowledge of physical laws? A phenomenon having been presented a number of times, with a particular character and in particular circumstances, we have judged that if this same phenomenon should occur in similar circumstances, it would have the same character;

that is to say, we have generalized the particular character of this phenomenon. Instead of descending from the general to the particular, we have ascended from the particular to the general. This general character is what we call a law: this law we have not deduced from a more general law or character; we have derived it from particular experiments in order to transfer it beyond them. It is not simple resumption nor a logical deduction; it is what we call induction. It is to induction that we owe all conquests over nature, all our discoveries of the laws of the world."

PROBLEM TO BE SOLVED.

This clear and eloquent exposition of the order of thought in the two processes of deduction and induction, as it has commonly been apprehended, enables us to present, without danger of being misunderstood, the problem which we wish to solve, namely, that there is no fundamental difference between induction and deduction; but in both cases the mind proceeds from the more general to the less general, or from the general to the particular; and that the opposite process of proceeding from the particular to the general is utterly impossible. All inference, I maintain, is of one kind—it is deductive. You may take as many particulars as you can gather together, and they will be perfectly barren of any consequence, unless you can attach them to a general principle. You may sum them up and call it generalization, but you can never infer a universal law, you can make no scientific generalization by means of them, unless you can put them upon some broader general principle than that which you wish to educe from them. Take the instance of scientific induction referred to by Cousin, that of the law of gravitation, and analyze it thoroughly, and you will see that it is at bottom deduction. A philosopher observes a material substance—a body—say, an apple, fall to the ground; he observes another body, a leaf, in like manner disengaging itself from the tree and following the apple; he casts a stone into the air, it takes the same direction; he casts a feather upon the winds, and, though for a time it is resisted by the currents of air, yet, when these obstacles cease, it directly in like manner falls to the earth. From these particulars he observes that it is the material substance in these different bodies that exhibits the phenomenon of falling to the earth, and not any particular quality of the apple, or the leaf, or the stone, or the feather; and this is his analysis. Thereupon he proceeds to infer that all bodies—all material substances—in all parts of the globe will behave in like manner; in other words, he infers the law of terrestrial gravity. This is his induction. He seems, indeed, merely to proceed from the particular to the general; but how? by what authority? on what ground? To answer this question is to solve the problem of inference.

DR. WHEWELL'S SOLUTION.

Dr. Whewell, who has elaborated this point, says that the conclusion is not a mere summing up of these particulars, and of all known particulars of the same nature; it is something more, a conception which, while it expresses these particulars, transcends them; it reaches all possible cases of the same kind. But how do we get this conception? He says we leap to it: "Induction mounts the ladder by a leap, which is out of the reach of method." But then it can turn round and verify itself by descending the ladder, step by step, by the deductive process. But how do we make the leap? By a sort of philosophical "sagacity— a scientific instinct—" which is the rare gift of some superior minds. But this explains nothing.

ANALYSIS OF INDUCTION, BY J. S. MILL.

Now, if this inference of the general law from observed particulars be a legitimate procedure, and it cannot admit of any solution, then it must be regarded as ultimate, and we may call it induction, and mark it as the opposite of deduction. But it happens that we can analyze the process in this instance and in all instances of induction; and this analysis will show that the subtle movement of the reasoning faculty from the particulars to the general is upon the broad basis of a universal and intuitive principle; and thus the whole process could easily be put into the form of a syllogism, with the principle for its major premise, and these observed particulars for its minor premise.

Happily the desired analysis of this process is furnished to our hand by Mr. Mill, who not only goes with Cousin in maintaining that induction is one fundamental mode of investigation, but advances far beyond him, contending with great ability that inference is always fundamentally from particulars to generals, and that deduction is only an intermediary process, which may be resorted to for convenience, but is of no avail for original discovery.

And here I can scarcely refrain from remarking how happily opposite systems conspire to advance the light of truth! By their conflict they bring to view the vital points of inquiry, and clear the ground for those who would approach to determine the merits of the case. If Mr. Mill has taken the wrong side of this question, yet it will ever be to his praise that his thorough comprehension of the subject and his precise and candid statements have placed the controversy in the clearest light; and if logicians differ it will not be because the point in dispute is misapprehended, but because their different systems of philosophy drive them to opposite conclusions. Hear what he says: "We must first observe that there is a principle implied in the very statement of what induction is, an assumption with regard to the course of nature and the order of the universe; namely, that there are such things as parallel cases, that what happens once will happen again, and not only again but always."—Vol. i, p. 370.

It is evident that Mr. Mill has thoroughly elaborated the opinion, for he has profoundly criticised the statement of it as made by Reid and Stewart, namely, that it is an intuitive conviction that the future will be as the present. He remarks: "Time, in its modification of past, present, or future, has nothing to do either with the belief itself or the grounds of it. We believe that fire will burn to-morrow, because it burned to-day and yesterday; but we believe on precisely the same grounds, that it burned before we were born, and that it burns at this very day in Cochin China. It is not from the past to the future, as past and future, that we infer, but from the known to the unknown, from facts observed to facts unobserved, from what we have perceived or have been directly conscious of, to what has not come within our experience. In this last predicament is the whole region of the future, but also the vastly greater portion of the present and the past."

THE ERROR OF MILL.

Thus far his criticism is just; but in what follows he denies that this principle is intuitive, and herein lies the whole error of his system. His empiricism forbids him to acknowledge that any universal principles, even the first principles of mathematics, are intuitive. He says: "Whatever be the most proper mode of expressing it, the proposition that the course of nature is uniform, is the fundamental principle or general axiom of induction. It would yet be a great error to consider this large generalization as any explanation of the inductive process. On the contrary, I hold it to be an instance of induction, and induction by no means of the most obvious kind. Far from being the first induction we make, it is one of the last, or, at all events, one of those which are latest in attaining strict philosophical accuracy. As a general maxim, indeed, it has scarcely entered the minds of any but philosophers, nor even by them, as we shall have many opportunities of remarking, have its extent and limits been always justly conceived. It is this principle, though so far from being our earliest induction, which must be considered as our warrant for all others in this sense, that unless it were true, all other inductions would be fallacious."

Thus this ingenious reasoner disclaims what he at first seemed to affirm. He disclaims making this principle any explanation of the process of induction as being founded upon it, or proceeding through it; but he now regards it as only the *sine qua non* of correct induction, so that no induction could be valid were its truth not admitted! And why? Because he thinks this principle is itself an induction, and that not the earliest in science. But if so, how could the earliest inductions have been made if their truth depends wholly upon this as their "fundamental principle?" And if itself be an induction how could it be made at all? It then must have been founded upon itself, or else here is one induction, and that the greatest of all, which is not formed on this principle. Good reason in these paralogisms to modify his statement! But take his qualified statement, that this late induction is the warrant of all other inductions, then it follows that all scientific inductions up to the time when this was formed, were without any warrant; and that warrant itself is without any warrant, except it be warranted by itself; and if this be impossible, then itself and all other inductions warranted by it are without authority!

But if we read on we shall find that what he calls " warrant in a certain sense" is what all who believe in deductive reasoning will call proof: "Archbishop Whately has well remarked that every induction is a syllogism, with the major premise suppressed; or, as I prefer to express it, that every induction may be thrown into the form of a syllogism by supplying a major premise. If this be actually done, the principle which we are now considering, that of the uniformity of the course of nature, will appear as the ultimate major premise of all inductions, and will, therefore, stand to all inductions in the relation in which, as has been shown at so much length, the major premise always stands to the conclusion, *not contributing at all to prove it*, but being a necessary condition of its being proved, since no conclusion is proved in which there cannot be found a true major premise."

But why will not Mr. Mill allow that a true major premise of a true syllogism proves its conclusion? Because the major premise contains the conclusion, and itself was formed by the addition of particulars, or induction from particulars of which that very conclusion was one. Passing this for the present, it is enough for our purpose that he admits that the principle of the uniform course of nature is the foundation of every induction in the very sense in which the major premise of a valid argument is the proof of its conclusion.

INDUCTION FOUNDED ON INTUITION.

The question now is, Where did we get that fundamental principle? It is absurd to consider it an induction, as we have seen, on Mr. Mill's own principles; it must then be a deduction or an intuition. It cannot be a deduction, for, as Mr. Mill has clearly seen, that would suppose a principle beyond it more general from which it was derived. It is an intuition, and is given by the reason in its primitive unfoldings, and on the very first occasion of the recurrence of any cause whose effect we have experienced, or of any cause similar to that primary cause. We see its manifestations in the very first rational actions of the child. Let the child put his finger upon a coal of fire, and he learns by experience that it causes pain. Can you get him voluntarily to touch it a second time? He sees another similar coal beside it; can you get him to touch that? He will no sooner touch the second than the first. Why not, seeing that he has no experience but that the first coal was once the cause of pain? He knows by experience nothing about its power to burn a second time, and nothing at all about the power of the second coal to burn. The only explanation is, that his reason obliges him to conclude as he does; and this law of the reason, this principle of mental order, when rendered into language, is the belief that like causes produce like effects. It is the province of the philosopher to look at this necessary movement of the reason and to abstract from it the axiom involved in it, and to lay it as the basis of all formal disquisitions upon the laws of nature. But the child is guided, nay, he is governed by it in all his future inductions. It transpires in the reason immediately after that great first principle of causality, that every event has a cause, which is as early as our first consciousness of sensation, and which is the occasion of our primitive ideas of the external world, and of God, the cause of causes, and lays the foundation of all science.

Nor is the principle of uniform causation in the human reason alone; it belongs as much to the instinct of animals of every grade—the fish, the bird, the insect, seems infallibly guided by it. It pervades the whole animated world, which without it, would rush on instant destruction. Indeed, the instinct of animals goes beyond this, and reveals the causative character of many objects before any experience can take place of their power to bless or to harm. It is not so with man; he must test everything himself, or be taught by those who have tested. A babe will as soon put his hand into a flame as snatch at a bouquet of flowers; he will chew the deadly herb as fearlessly as the lamb would pluck the tender grass.

HUME'S OPINION.

This fact has been noticed by Mr. Hume with an eagerness which characterizes his devotion to empiricism. He then takes occasion to wonder, with an air of delighted skepticism, how it is, after learning thus the particular character of causes, we can infer they will continue to produce the same effects.

"All our reasoning on matters of fact seems to be founded on cause and effect. By means of this relation alone we can go beyond the evidence of our memory and senses. If you were to ask a man why he believes any matter of fact which is absent; for instance, that his friend is in the country or in France, he would give you a reason, and this reason would be some other fact, as a letter received from him, or a knowledge of his former resolution. A man finding a watch, or any other machine, on a desert island, would conclude that there had once been men in that island. All our reasonings concerning facts are of the same nature. . . . If we would satisfy ourselves, therefore, concerning the nature of that evidence which assures of matters of fact, we must inquire how we came at the knowledge of cause and effect. I shall venture to affirm, as a general proposition, which admits of no exception, that the knowledge of this is *not in any instance attained by reasonings a priori, but arises entirely from experience*, when we find any particular objects are conjoined with each other.

Let any object be presented to a man of ever so strong natural reason and abilities, if that object be entirely new to him, he will not be able by the most accurate examination of its sensible qualities to discover any of its causes or effects. Adam, though his rational faculties be supposed at the very first entirely perfect, could not have inferred from the fluidity and transparency of water that it would suffocate him, or from the light and warmth of fire that it would consume him."

All this we see no reason to dispute; but when he advances to the conclusion that it is by repeated or customary experiences that we discover the uniformity of causation, we find him as blind to the real working of the human reason as he would be blind to the operation of animal instincts if he should affirm that all animals, like man, discover all noxious food and other hurtful causes by experience. But let Mr. Hume speak for himself upon this point: "As to past experience, it can be allowed to give direct and certain information of those precise objects only and that precise period of time which fell under its experience; but why this experience should extend to future times and to other objects, which, for aught we know, may be only in appearance similar; this is the main question on which I insist. The bread which I formerly ate nourished me; that is, a body of such sensible qualities has induced secret powers. But does it follow that other bread must also nourish me at another time, and that like sensible qualities must always be attended with like secret powers? The consequence seems to be no wise necessary. At least it must be acknowledged that there is here a consequence drawn by the mind, that there is a certain step taken, a process of thought, or inference, which wants to be explained. These two propositions are far from being the same. I have found that such an object has always been attended with such an effect, and I foresee that other objects, which are in appearance similar, will be attended with similar effects. I shall allow, if you please, that one proposition may justly be inferred from the other. I know, in fact, that it always is inferred. But if you insist that the inference is made by a chain of reasoning, I desire you to produce that reasoning."

Eureka! good Mr. Hume, we have found out

that reasoning, that connecting principle which you despaired of finding. It lay just before your eyes when you penned the observation that one proposition is always inferred from the other. Do you not see that you here struck upon a law of the reason by which it is necessitated to operate thus, and that this law expressed in language is the axiom, Like causes produce like effects? or, as it is generally stated, The course of nature is uniform. What men always think and must think is a primary and essential truth, an ultimate principle of reason.

But Mr. Hume has objected to this origin of the principle. "Were it the offspring of the reason, an intuition, it would be as perfect at first and from one instance, as after ever so long a course of experience. But the case is far otherwise. Nothing is so like as eggs; yet no one, on account of this apparent similarity, expects the same taste and relish in all of them. It is only after a long course of experiments in any kind that we attain a firm reliance and security with regard to a particular event. Now, where is that process of reasoning which from one instance draws a conclusion so different from that which it infers from a hundred instances, that are nowise different from that single one? This question I propose as much for the sake of instruction as with an intention of raising difficulties. I cannot find, I cannot imagine any such reasoning."

It would be easy to turn off this question with a joke, especially as the example of the eggs is so egregiously puerile; but it is due to the candor of Mr. Hume to treat it seriously, nay, to admit that the question is one of great importance, and leads to the true science of induction. It is not true that bodies having the same or similar qualities produce different effects; the eggs that have a different taste are different in some particulars, and this is usually sufficiently manifest in eggs; and if your eyes fail to see it, a microscope will abundantly reveal it. Just here opens to our view the appropriate sphere of induction, as far as it may be properly distinguished from deduction; its office is to analyze phenomena, to mark the different qualities of objects, and to ascertain their precise effects; but when you have certainly determined what qualities in any case produce what effects, one single instance of causation is sufficient for the widest generalization. Show me the property of the magnet which attracts iron, and I hesitate not to predict that whenever and wherever that quality appears, in like circumstances, it will be followed by the same effect. But if I have not been careful in my observations and mistaken some other property for the real one, then most certainly I shall make a false prediction, and the event will expose the error. It is not in the reason, which assures me intuitively that like causes produce like effects, but in my observation.

MERIT OF MILL.

Science is under no greater obligation to any writer of the present age than to Mr. John Stuart Mill, for the profound and elaborate exposition of the grounds and process of induction which he has given to the world. "There is no event," he remarks, "happening in the universe, which is not connected by an invariable sequence with some one or more of the phenomena which preceded it." "If we knew all the agents which exist at the present moment, their collocation in space, and their properties, or in other words, the laws or modes of their agency, we could predict the whole subsequent history of the universe; at least, unless some new volition of a power capable of controlling the universe should supervene. And if any particular state of the universe should ever recur a second time, (which, however, all experience combines to assure us will never happen,) all subsequent states would return too, and history would, like a circulating decimal of many figures, periodically repeat itself.

> "Jam redit et virgo, redeunt Saturnia regna,
> Alter erit tum Tiphys, et altera quæ vehat Argo
> Delectos heroas: erunt quoque altera bella,
> Atque iterum ad Troiam magnus mittetur Achilles."

Such undoubtedly is the order of the universe, with the single exception of the free-will of moral agents. But Mr. Mill makes no such exception, for he holds that human volitions are so far controlled by motives that a man's actions as inevitably result from his character as any effect follows a cause; and if we thoroughly knew his character we could certainly predict how he would act in any supposable case. But this we repudiate, for this reason, among many which cannot now be mentioned, that the same view must apply to the divine mind; and then it would follow that the universe, like a circulating decimal, actually has been, and will be produced and destroyed, again and again, forever. For God is the same in character; and if, when nothing was but he, his power produced the present universe, it was but the type of a past and a coming eternity. Plato's reminiscences are resurrections; and not only the ideas that now are have been before, but we ourselves, the world's millions, and all their various histories, have been before as now, and will be as they now are, again and again, forevermore. But, aside from free agents, the idea of Mr. Mill is as true as it is sublime; and it illuminates and explains the problem of induction. The law of causation binds together the universe, and the only difficulty is to discover that chain amid the shifting, and veering, and multitudinous phenomena that move about it and upon it; but if you can strike that chain at one point it will vibrate throughout its whole direction. "The order of nature, as perceived at first glance, presents at every instant a chaos, followed by another chaos. We must decompose each chaos into single facts. We must learn to see in the chaotic antecedent a multitude of distinct antecedents, and in the chaotic consequent a multitude of distinct consequents." What then? We have to determine which particular antecedent is followed by which consequent, and which consequent is produced by which antecedent; then, by the simplest ratiocination, whose major premise is the principle of causality, furnished by the reason, we generalize the fact, or, in other words, infer a law of nature. To make the requisite analysis we need to observe and experiment; and we require no aid but the simple rules of arithmetic, except in those cases where the effects of various causes are mixed together, as the curvilinear motion of the rocket, which is the result of various causes. Here we require the aid of the higher mathematics to determine the proportion in which the causes mingle in producing the effect. But all mathematics is deductive. Hence, nowhere in induction, throughout its whole circuit, can you find any new principle of inference. Inference, therefore, is always one and the same; it is a passage of the thought from the more general to the less general, or to the particular; and never *vice versa*, from the particular or from particulars, however numerous, to the general. I repeat, you may sum them up, and call them by a general name; but that is no inference, no induction, nothing but generalization.

CONCLUSION OF THE ARGUMENT.

Thus, it is demonstrated that the process by which we discover the laws of nature is fundamentally a deductive process; and that we are as much indebted to the reason for the major premise as we are indebted to experience for the minor premise.

ARISTOTLE VINDICATED.

It is owing to a misapprehension of the intuitive developments of the reason that some modern philosophers have rejected the syllogism as a type of ratiocination. They suppose its major premise is a general truth obtained by a summation of particulars; and, consequently, to deduce one of these particulars from the general is to reason in a circle. But, great as the mystery of the reason may appear, we hold it to be the source of general principles, and it gives them to us as by revelation. So struck was Cousin with this function of reason that he seemed well-nigh beside himself, and almost ready to bow down and worship it as a portion of divinity; and Plato, at the dawn of philosophy, declared, "It is the gift of the gods to man, which, as I conceive, they sent down by some Prometheus in a blaze of light." But it is no enthusiasm to say that the reason is the brightest aspect of the image of God in man. Were the human mind destitute of this power of intuition it would be impossible to vindicate the logic of Aristotle. This he clearly saw and stated in his exposition of the process of deduction. Indemonstrable truths, he affirms, make the basis of all reasoning; for if your premises be demonstrated, then they must have been demonstrated by something beyond them, and if they were demonstrable though not demonstrated, it only extends the chain indefinitely back. Hence there must be indemonstrable truths at the foundation of every reasoning process, or it is without foundation. And these indemonstrable truths are particular intuitions of sense, of consciousness, and of the reason, and also the general intuitions or principles of the reason. Thus sense gives us direct knowledge of the qualities of bodies; consciousness, of the phenomena of mind; and reason, ideas of substance, space, time, cause, right and wrong, and the principles of causality, mathematical principles, etc. The principle of contradiction, namely, a thing cannot be and not be at the same time, Aristotle considered the first of these indemonstrable principles, which lay at the foundation of demonstration.

ERROR OF THE SCHOOLMEN.

The error of the schoolmen, which plunged them into the vortex of abstract speculation, and for which Plato is to be blamed rather than Aristotle, was in the supposition that all truth lay wrapped up in *a priori* principles, and could be educed by ratiocination: they failed to perceive that they yielded no consequences of scientific value, but as they were attached to facts. Bacon reclaimed science from folly by turning her eye upon the actual phenomena of nature. But it is an illusion as great as that of the scholastics, to suppose that facts can of themselves give science; for they are as inconsequential without the principles of intuition as these are barren without them; they lie scattered about like pebbles on the shore, until they are bound together by some *a priori* principle or general truth; then we see in them the path of the mighty laws that clasp and encircle the universe. A falling apple sheds a ray of light through immensity, and a drop of rain marking the clay pours its illuminations down the chasms of a past eternity.

And is not here the answer to Mr. Mill's earnest inquiry: "Why is a single instance in some cases sufficient for a complete induction; while in others, myriads of concurring instances, without a single exception, known or presumed, go so little way toward establishing a universal proposition?" The difference in the cases is that the former stands in the relation of cause and effect, and the latter does not. "Whoever," he adds, "can answer this question knows more than the wisest of the ancients, and has solved the problem of induction." Let him add the true theory of the origin of primary axioms to his own incomparable analysis of induction, and he may demand the palm. Take away the *a priori* principles from induction, and you cover with clouds the whole process, and the long array of the sciences dependent upon it;

restore these ideas and the movement is attended with certainty, as far as certainty can belong to human knowledge.

I say as far as certainty belongs to human knowledge, because, after all, it must be confessed that absolute knowledge is not for man. In its very depths what is our knowledge but faith? When we talk of certainty what do we mean? Certainty for an individual is but his necessary belief; human certainty is the necessary and universal belief of the race. In heaven itself certainty is absolute only in the Throne of Light; the knowledge of the loftiest archangel nearest that Throne is but a cloudless belief, forced upon his understanding by its own subjective laws. God only knows, and knows he knows; God only is light.

SECOND CAUSES.

This leads us to remark, that the problem of induction being only a question of causation, it matters not what theory any one adopts in respect to second causes, if he admits that no event is without a cause, and like causes produce like effects, that is, what seems to us to be causes. To me, however, there is no more difficulty in supposing that God has put a causative power in nature distinct from his own, than that he has constituted nature, both matter and mind, distinct from his own essence. If matter exists with its various elements distinct from the divine nature, though not independent of it, why may we not suppose that God has endued it with a motive property as well as other properties? Secondary causes are the general belief of mankind as well as secondary natures. Still, you may take either hypothesis; you may think it was the electric fluid which struck the oak when it fell, blasted and blazing with lightning, or you may regard it as the stroke of the divine thought or volition, and think that all other events are, in like manner, the extemporaneous movements of the all-pervading mind of Deity. Yet if your reason obliges you to believe that they proceed upon the principles of causality, then induction is the same, and the certainty of its results is the same. Proceeding upon *a priori* and empirical data conjointly, the process is not to be doubted until the faculties of observation and reason are doubted; and when they are doubted the mind is ruined, and the light of knowledge is set forever.

II.

MISCELLANEOUS EXAMPLES FOR PRACTICE.

LESSON I.

1. That which is followed by repentance is not to be desired;
Some pleasures are followed by repentance;
Therefore, some pleasures are not to be desired.
2. If the world existed from eternity there would be records prior to the Mosaic; and if it were produced by chance it would not bear marks of design;
But there are no records prior to the Mosaic, and the world does not bear marks of design; therefore,
The world neither existed from eternity, nor is it the work of chance.
3. Every dispensation of Providence is beneficial;
Afflictions are dispensations of Providence;
Therefore, they are beneficial.

4. If there is a God he ought to be worshiped;
    But there is a God;
    Therefore, he ought to be worshiped.
5. If God is infinitely wise, and acts with perfect freedom, he does nothing but what is best;
    But God is infinitely wise, and acts with perfect freedom;
    Therefore, he does nothing but what is best.
6. If God were not a Being of infinite goodness, neither would he consult the happiness of his creatures;
    But God does consult the happiness of his creatures;
    Therefore, he is a Being of infinite goodness.
7. The world is either self-existent, or the work of some finite, or of some infinite being;
    But it is not self-existent, nor the work of a finite being;
    Therefore, it is the work of an infinite Being.
8. No deceitful man merits confidence;
    All honest men merit confidence;
    Therefore, no honest man is deceitful.

9. Every human virtue is to be sought with diligence;
Prudence is a human virtue;
Therefore, prudence is to be sought diligently.
10. Everything base should be avoided;
Some pleasures are base;
Therefore, some pleasures should be avoided.

LESSON II.

1. He who follows evil counsel will meet with trouble;
Rehoboam followed evil counsel;
Therefore, Rehoboam met with trouble.
2. No good citizen will violate the laws of God and man;
Duelists do that which violates the laws of both God and man;
Therefore, duelists are not good citizens.
3. Things offensive to delicacy should not be used;
Therefore, some words should not be used.
4. That which is prudent is commendable;
Moderation is prudent;
Therefore, moderation is commendable.

5. We are bound to set apart one day in seven for religious duties, if the fourth commandment is obligatory on us; but we are bound to set apart one day in seven for religious duties; and hence it appears that the fourth commandment is obligatory on us.

6. A desire to gain by another's loss is a violation of the tenth commandment; all gaming, therefore, since it implies a desire to profit at the expense of another, involves a breach of the tenth commandment.

7. All the fish that the net inclosed were an indiscriminate mixture of various kinds; those that were set aside and saved as valuable, were fish that the net inclosed; therefore, those that were set aside and saved as valuable were an indiscriminate mixture of various kinds.

8. No one who lives with another on terms of confidence is justified on any pretense in killing him; Brutus lived on terms of confidence with Cesar; therefore, he was not justified, on the pretense he pleaded, in killing him.

9. Seeing that I have experienced calamity in the snares of pleasure, I should abandon its pursuit.
10. The principles of justice are variable; the appointments of nature are invariable; therefore, the principles of justice are no appointment of nature.

LESSON III.

1. All good Christians are saved;
All good Christians have sinned;
Therefore, some who have sinned will be saved.
2. Knowledge is better than riches;
Virtue is better than knowledge;
Therefore, virtue is better than riches.
3. Christianity requires us to believe what the apostles wrote;
St. Paul is an apostle;
Therefore, Christianity requires us to believe what St. Paul wrote.
4. It is necessary that a general should understand the art of war;
But Caius did not understand the art of war;
Therefore, it is necessary that Caius should not be a general.

5. A total eclipse of the sun would cause darkness at noon;
It is possible that the moon at that time may totally eclipse the sun;
Therefore, it is possible that the moon may cause darkness at noon.
6. The fogs vanish as the sun rises;
But the fogs have not yet begun to vanish;
Therefore, the sun is not yet risen.
7. The sun is a senseless being;
What the Persians worshiped is the sun;
Therefore, what the Persians worshiped is a senseless being.
8. If every creature be reasonable every brute is reasonable;
But no brute is reasonable;
Therefore, no creature is reasonable.

LESSON IV.

1. God is omnipotent;
An omnipotent being can do everything possible;
He that can do everything possible can do whatever involves not a contradiction;
Therefore, God can do whatever involves not a contradiction.

2. If we love any person, all emotions of hatred toward him cease;

If all emotions of hatred toward a person cease, we cannot rejoice in his misfortunes;

If we rejoice not in his misfortunes, we certainly wish him no injury;

Therefore, if we love a person we wish him no injury.

3. A thinking substance is a spirit;
A spirit has no extension;
What has no extension has no parts;
What has no parts is indissoluble;
Therefore, the mind is immortal.

4. If God did not create the world perfect in its kind, it must either proceed from want of inclination or from want of power;

But it could not proceed from want of inclination or from want of power;

Therefore, God created the world perfect in its kind, or, which is the same thing, it is absurd to say that he did not create the world perfect in its kind.

5. Whatever is immaterial is indissoluble;
The mind of man is immaterial;
Therefore, the mind of man is indissoluble.

6. Whatever perceives, judges, and reasons, is a thinking substance;

The human mind perceives, judges, and reasons;

Therefore, the human mind is a thinking substance.

7. Things equal to the same thing are equal to one another;

Therefore, these two triangles, each equal to the square of a line of three inches, are equal between themselves.

8. What is not a being, since it can have no attributes, can be no agent nor act, cannot produce anything;

What is called nothing is not a being, has no attribute, is not an agent, nor can it act; therefore, what is called nothing cannot act or produce anything.

9. The order and constitution of things established and maintained in the universe, is the law of Supreme intelligence;

Nature is the order and constitution of things established and maintained in the universe; therefore,

Nature is the law of Supreme intelligence.

LESSON V.

1. No man can possess power to perform impossibilities;
A miracle is an impossibility;
Therefore, no man can possess power to perform a miracle.

2. War is the source of numerous evils;
Some wars are just; therefore,
Some just actions are the source of numerous evils.

3. Protection from punishment is plainly due to the innocent; therefore, as you maintain that this person ought not to be punished, it appears that you are convinced of his innocence.

4. All the most bitter persecutions have been religious persecutions; among the most bitter persecutions were those which occurred in France during the Revolution; therefore, they must have been religious persecutions.

5. Of two evils the less is to be preferred; occasional turbulence, therefore, being a less evil than rigid despotism, is to be preferred to it.

6. The early and general assignment of the Epistle to the Hebrews to St. Paul as its author, must have been either from its professing to be his, and containing his name, or from its really being his; since, therefore, the former of these is not the fact, the epistle must be Paul's.
7. All the miracles of Jesus would fill more books than the world could contain; the things related by the evangelists are the miracles of Jesus; therefore, the things related by the evangelists would fill more books than the world could contain.
8. According to theologians, a man must possess faith in order to be acceptable to the Deity; now he who believes all the fables of the Hindoo mythology must possess faith; therefore, such a one must, according to theologians, be acceptable to the Deity.
9. If Abraham were justified, it must have been either by faith or by works; now, he was not justified by faith, (according to St. James,) nor by works, (according to St. Paul;) therefore, Abraham was not justified.

10. He who cannot possibly act otherwise than he does has neither merit nor demerit in his action; a liberal and benevolent man cannot possibly act otherwise than he does in relieving the poor; therefore, such a man has neither merit nor demerit in his action.

LESSON VI.

1. Smollet, in a town in France, having met at an inn with a scolding chambermaid and an awkward red-haired hostler, who had engrossed his whole attention, immediately wrote in his journal: "The men in this town are all red-haired, and the women are all scolds."

2. The Stoics proved that the world was a great animal, thus: That which has the use of reason is better than that which has not. Now, there is nothing better than the world; therefore, the world has reason and is a great animal.

3. The Sophists used the following argument against marriage: If a woman that marries be lovely she will create jealousies; if she be ugly she will not delight; therefore, it is not good to marry.

4. An Irishman, hearing much of the charms of a feather bed, took a feather and laid it on a rock for a pillow. He awoke with a headache. "Arrah," said he, "if these be your feathers give me my straw."

5. Warm countries alone produce the Banian-tree. Spain is a warm country; therefore, Spain produces the Banian-tree.

6. A canal boat was passing under a bridge, and some one on deck cried out, "Look out!" A Dutchman lying in his berth heard the cry, and stuck his head out of the window, and received a severe blow on his forehead. "Vat for," cried he, in a passion, "did you tell me to 'look out?' vy did you not tell me to 'look in?'"

7. As I would not trifle with the prejudices of the poor, because it is illiberal, so I would not always yield to them, because it is unwise.

8. Books are seldom correct, because human nature is fallible.

9. Fugitive cant, which is always in a state of increase or decay, cannot be regarded as any part of the durable materials of a language, and therefore must be suffered to perish with other things unworthy of preservation.

10. Pleasures are deceitful; therefore, young men should curb their inclinations.

LESSON VII.

Let the learner analyze the following, giving,
1st, the terms; 2d, the propositions; 3d, the syllogisms.

Ye men of Athens, I perceive that in all things ye are too superstitious. For as I passed by and beheld your devotions I found an altar with this inscription: "To the Unknown God." Whom, therefore, ye ignorantly worship him declare I unto you. God that made the world and all things therein, seeing that he is Lord of heaven and earth, dwelleth not in temples made with hands; neither is worshiped with men's hands, as though he needed anything, seeing he giveth to all life, and breath, and all things; and hath made of one blood all nations of men for to dwell on all the face of the earth, and hath determined the times before appointed, and the bounds of their habitation; that they should seek the Lord, if haply they might feel after him and find him, though he be not far from every one of us:

For in him we live, and move, and have our being; as certain, also, of your own poets have said, for we are also his offspring.

Forasmuch, then, as we are the offspring of God, we ought not to think that the Godhead is like unto gold, or silver, or stone, graven by art and man's device.

And the times of this ignorance God winked at, but now commandeth all men everywhere to repent;

Because he hath appointed a day in the which he will judge the world in righteousness by that man whom he hath ordained; whereof he hath given assurance unto all men in that he hath raised him from the dead.

LESSON VIII.

Arguments from unpublished documents.

1. If the Mosaic doctrine of the absolute creation of the world out of nothing, by the divine decree, were unreasonable, it would have shocked the common mind.
2. If Pantheism be true, and all things are but a development of the Deity, then the idea of *cause* in the human mind is an il-

lusion, for in that case it is nowhere fully realized, as modifications are not absolute causations.

3. Though we cannot, with Plato and Cousin, regard the reason in man as itself divine, it is certainly perfect; and is, therefore, as a perfect creation, evidence of a perfect Creator.

4. No interpretation of the Bible is to be considered correct which is directly opposed to the absolute principles of reason, for this would be suicidal, inasmuch as every argument for the divine inspiration of the Bible is based upon those very principles.

5. If the New Testament be not a true history of Christ, it is the greatest romance in all literature; and if it be the greatest romance ever written, its author could not have been unknown to his cotemporaries.

6. If the story of the resurrection be true, the Christian religion is proved to be of divine origin; if it be false, no explanation can be given of the sudden and extensive spread of the Christian faith.

7. The Bible must be of divine origin, for its production is beyond all example of human genius.

The remainder are from notes of Dr. Whedon.

8. Every necessary, universal, and perpetual idea is a truth;
Immortality is such an idea;
Therefore, immortality is a truth.

9. Nothing is to be held eternal which we can rationally conceive once to have not existed, and the infinite space to be vacant of it.

10. Nothing is by the laws of the mind to be held as having no beginning, which we can rationally conceive to have once nonexisted and then begun. Now of the visible material world we can conceive space to have been empty, we can conceive that it once nonexisted and then began. Not so of space or of creative mind. In order to the world's beginning, these must have preceded and never have had a beginning.

11. The regular organization of the world must either be eternal, or formed without design, or formed by design;

The regular organization of the world cannot be eternal; for geology shows it to be composed of elements once inorganic.

The regular organism of the world cannot be without design, for no complex adjustment of parts to accomplish an end can exist without design.

12. The regular organization of the world is by design, for it accords with all the laws of design, and with nothing else that we know.

LESSON IX.

Supposed Exceptions to Rules.

Hamilton, Thompson, and our own countryman, Mahan, and others, have suggested several alterations in the forms of Logic, as left by Aristotle; but with deference to these original thinkers, I consider them unnecessary and inexpedient. To try the skill of the advanced student, and to make this book as complete as may be, without an adequate discussion of these topics, the present lesson will contain

EXAMPLES FOR PRACTICE. 169

specimens of those propositions and arguments which have been supposed to be exceptions to the rules and to require a re-formation of the science.

Eight Classes of Propositions, instead of the four, A, E, I, O, of Aristotle.

1. Toto-total. All A is all of B.—All men are all rational animals.
2. Toto-partial. All A is some of B.—All men are mortal.
3. Parti-total. Some A is all of B.—Some men are all the sailors.
4. Parti-partial. Some A is some of B.—Some men are sailors.
5. Toto-total. Any A is not any B.—No man is a brute.
6. Toto-partial. Any A is not some B.—No man is some brute.
7. Parti-total. Some A is not any B.—Some men are no brutes.
8. Parti-partial. Some A is not some B.—Some men are not some brutes.

Thompson makes but six.

A. All plants grow.
E. No right action is inexpedient.

I. Some muscles act without volition.
O. Some plants do not grow in the tropics.
U. Common salt is chloride of sodium.
Y. Some stars are all planets.

Hamilton and Mahan add:

ω. Some X is not some Y.
η. No X is some Z.

A is converted into Y.
E   "   "   E.
I   "   "   I.
O   "   "   η.
U   "   "   U.
Y   "   "   A.

ω   "   "   ω.
η   "   "   O.

If we admit Sir William Hamilton's doctrine of the *Quantification of the Predicate*, namely, that if you refer not to the form of expression, but to what is meant by it, the *predicate has always a definite quantity, and the proposition may always be converted simply;* still this very difference between the form of a proposition and its meaning, makes it necessary to have rules to determine what is the extent of the predicate and to govern conversion; and no rules are better than those of Aristotle, if we keep in mind the exceptions to the rules I have made. (See Section on Distribution.)

EXAMPLES OF IMMEDIATE INFERENCE.

These supposed inferences will be found to be either the same as the premise in different language, or derived from it by means of another premise understood, or by conversion.

IMMEDIATE INFERENCE BY MEANS OF PRIVATIVE CONCEPTIONS.

I. The Premise, a Positive Conception.

A. All the righteous are happy;
 Therefore, none of the righteous are unhappy;
 And, all who are unhappy are unrighteous.
E. No human virtues are perfect;
 Therefore, all human virtues are imperfect;
 And, all perfect virtues are not human.
I. Some possible cases are probable;
 Therefore, some possible cases are not improbable;
 And, some probable cases are not impossible.

O. Some possible cases are not probable;
Therefore, some possible cases are improbable;
And, some improbable cases are not impossible.

U. The just are [all] the holy;
Therefore, all unholy men are unjust;
And, no just men are unholy.

Y. Some happy persons are [all] the righteous;
Therefore, all who are unhappy are unrighteous;
And, no righteous persons are unhappy.

II. The Premise, a Privative Conception.

A. All the insincere are dishonest;
Therefore, no insincere man is honest;
And, all honest men are sincere.

E. No unjust act is unpunished;
Therefore, all unjust acts are punished;
And, all acts not punished are just.

I. Some unfair acts are unknown;
Therefore, some unfair acts are not known;
And, some unknown acts are not fair.

O. Some improbable cases are not impossible;
Therefore, some improbable cases are possible;
And, some possible cases are not probable.

U. The unlawful is the [only] inexpedient;
Therefore, the lawful is the expedient;
And the lawful is not the inexpedient.

Y. Some unhappy men are [all] the unrighteous;
Therefore, no happy men are unrighteous;
And, some unhappy men are not righteous.

IMMEDIATE INFERENCE BY ADDED DETERMINANTS.

A servant is a fellow-creature;

Therefore, a servant in suffering is a fellow-creature in suffering.

Virtue deserves respect, and a servant is a fellow-creature;

Therefore, a virtuous servant is a fellow-creature deserving of respect.

IMMEDIATE INFERENCE BY COMPLEX CONCEPTION.

Oxygen is an element, so that the decomposition of oxygen would be the decomposition of an element.

IMMEDIATE INFERENCES OF INTERPRETATION.

All the Gentiles are also called; that is, all other nations, as well as the Jewish, are called.

Howard exhibited this high philanthropic spirit;

Therefore, such philanthropy really exists.

A is B; therefore, B exists.

A is B; therefore, where A is we find B.

IMMEDIATE INFERENCE FROM A DISJUNCTIVE JUDGMENT.

All teeth are either incisors, canine, bicuspid, or molar;

Therefore, the molar teeth are neither incisors, canine, nor bicuspid;

And, all teeth which are not molar are either canine, incisors, or bicuspid.

IMMEDIATE INFERENCE BY THE SUM OF SEVERAL PREDICATES.

Copper is a metal of a red color and disagreeable smell and taste, all the properties of which are poisonous; which is highly malleable, ductile, tenacious, with a specific gravity of about 8.83;

Therefore, a metal of a red color, etc., is copper.

UNFIGURED SYLLOGISM.

In the unfigured syllogism of Hamilton and Mahan the terms compared do not stand to each other in the relation of subject and predicate, being in the same proposition either *both subjects or both predicates.*

All C and some B are equal;
All A and all B are equal;
Therefore, all C and some A are equal;
Or, C and A are unequal.

Copperas and sulphate of iron are identical;
Sulphate of iron and sulphate of copper are not identical;
Therefore, copperas and sulphate of copper are not identical.

All C and all B equal Y;
All A and all B do not equal Y;
Therefore, C and A are not equal to each other.

C and B always coexist, or are universally compatible;

A and B never coexist, or are wholly incompatible;

Therefore, C and A never coexist, or are not compatible.

Some of these unfigured syllogisms, upon analysis, will be found to contain one or two other syllogisms with premises suppressed. In the first instance given, "*Things equal to the same thing are equal to each other*," is the implied premise.

REASONING FROM WHOLES IN COMPREHENSION.

Sir William Hamilton's discovery is illusory; an individual cannot comprehend a species, nor a species a genus. *This red rose* is both in extension and comprehension *one*. A single rose with its own red; it cannot comprehend *red rose*, which is not *only this, but that, and all other red roses;* and it admits of no inference. A thing is itself and not something else however like it, much less its class. So *triangle comprehends* not *figure*, but only the *three-angled portion*.

THE END.

www.ingramcontent.com/pod-product-compliance
Lightning Source LLC
Chambersburg PA
CBHW032157160426
43197CB00008B/957